9780498073724

Oakland Community College
Orchard Ridge Campus Library
27055 Orchard Lake Road
Farmington, Michigan 48024

The Films
of
James Stewart

Mr. McClure is the author of *The Truman Administration and the Problems of Postwar Labor*

Mr. McClure and Mr. Twomey are the co-authors of *The Versatiles*

The Films of
James Stewart

by

Ken D. Jones
Arthur F. McClure
Alfred E. Twomey

CASTLE BOOKS ★ **NEW YORK**

© 1970 by A. S. Barnes and Co., Inc.
Library of Congress Catalogue Card Number: 70-88284

This Edition Published by Arrangement
with A. S. Barnes & Co., Inc.

Printed in the United States of America

To Mr. Smith———

who went to Washington

a number of years ago.

Contents

Foreword by Henry Fonda 9
Preface 13
James Stewart: The Sober Enthusiast 17
Murder Man 25
Rose Marie 27
Next Time We Love 28
Wife Versus Secretary 31
Small Town Girl 33
Speed 34
The Gorgeous Hussy 36
Born To Dance 39
After the Thin Man 41
Seventh Heaven 44
The Last Gangster 48
Navy Blue and Gold 50
Of Human Hearts 53
Vivacious Lady 56
Shopworn Angel 59
You Can't Take It With You 61
Made For Each Other 65
Ice Follies of 1939 68
It's a Wonderful World 70
Mr. Smith Goes to Washington 73
Destry Rides Again 76
The Shop Around the Corner 80
The Mortal Storm 84
No Time For Comedy 87
The Philadelphia Story 90
Come Live With Me 94
Pot O'Gold 97
Ziegfeld Girl 99
It's a Wonderful Life 103
Magic Town 106
Call Northside 777 109
On Our Merry Way 113
Rope 115
You Gotta Stay Happy 118
The Stratton Story 122
Malaya 125
Winchester '73 128
Broken Arrow 131
The Jackpot 134
Harvey 138
No Highway in the Sky 142
The Greatest Show on Earth 145
Bend of the River 149
Carbine Williams 152
The Naked Spur 155
Thunder Bay 158
The Glenn Miller Story 162
Rear Window 166
The Far Country 170
Strategic Air Command 175
The Man from Laramie 178
The Man Who Knew Too Much 183
The Spirit of St. Louis 186
Night Passage 189
Vertigo 193
Bell, Book and Candle 196
Anatomy of a Murder 200
The FBI Story 204
The Mountain Road 207
Two Rode Together 211
X-15 214
The Man Who Shot Liberty Valance 215
Mr. Hobbs Takes a Vacation 219
How the West Was Won 223
Take Her, She's Mine 227
Cheyenne Autumn 230

Dear Brigitte 233
Shenandoah 237
Flight of the Phoenix 240
The Rare Breed 244
Firecreek 248
Bandolero! 251
A Selected Bibliography 254

Foreword

by

HENRY FONDA

The thing of it is Jim really became an actor in spite of himself. Jim has already earned about all the honors an actor and a man can expect in a lifetime. Let me suggest how it happened as I saw it.

Jim was an architect major at Princeton, class of '32. He was in the Triangle Show his senior year, played the lanky leading man, the accordion, and sang some.

He accepted the invitation to join the University Players on Cape Cod the summer after graduation because he knew from friends that it would be a fun-filled, exciting eight weeks and something to do before he went home to Indiana, Pennsylvania. We hadn't met yet; actually he was filling the vacancy created by my leaving the Players for what I thought would be more promising summer stock work. And I didn't see Jim during that summer, but I know it was the fun he expected and there was an added fillip—a play tried out at Falmouth was brought to New York in the early fall with the cast intact and Jim had a small role. The play was *Carrie Nation* with Esther Dale in the title role and also carried Mildred Natwick, Joshua Logan, Bretaigne Windust, Myron McCormick, among others to Broadway.

I was playing stock in East Orange, New Jersey, commuting from New York, and Josh and Mack and Jim and I took an apartment on West 64th Street to share expenses. I think we were earning an average of 50 or 60 dollars a week, and I remember we paid 80 dollars a month for a furnished two-room and kitchen apartment.

Well, *Carrie Nation* closed after three or four weeks and Jim got ready to go home, not at all discouraged. You could see he was looking forward to the stories he could tell his family and friends. He'd been in a play on Broadway! Who'd have ever thought? You know—"Look ma, no hands!"

Well, before he quite got packed Arthur Beckhard, the producer of *Carrie Nation* announced another play, in which there was a small part for Jim. He hadn't tried to get it, it just fell that way. Josh was stage manager, and there was another small part for Mac.

Henry Fonda

I should emphasize here, if I haven't made the point that Josh and Mac and I knew we wanted to make it professionally in the theatre.

So Jim stayed on and *Good-Bye Again,* with Osgood Perkins, was a hit. And Jim was on stage about a minute and a half and got three laughs. I graduated from East Orange to a small part in a

Foreword

Tallulah Bankhead play and *I* got three laughs.

So the 1932–33 season rolled on and *Good-Bye Again* finally closed. And Jim starts to pack again and somebody calls and Jim gets a part in *All Good Americans*. They needed an actor who could play an accordion, and like Jim had a monopoly there.

So we're into the season of '33–34. The thing is, you see, when you're a young unknown actor, you spend your days tramping Times Square, the casting offices, agents, producers. Not Jim. This was all some kind of big mistake—not like he'd planned at all.

Someplace in there we moved to the Madison Square Hotel. Josh was on a trip to Russia and Mac was up to something else. And someplace in there Jim took a long slow look around him and at himself and began to think maybe he'd blundered into something pretty good. I'd seen him in these plays and he was always good. You know, he was pleasant, and funny, and had his own charm. He was my friend, and I was proud of him. But the parts were all small and undemanding.

Then he got a good part as Judith Anderson's son in *Divided By Three*. I went to the opening night and afterward in his dressing room I remember just sitting looking at him and studying him and wondering how the hell he got to be so good! You see, I'd been at it for eight or nine years already playing literally hundreds of parts of all kinds and really working at being an actor—and here was this skinny son-of-a-bitch who hadn't really tried very hard for maybe a year or so and I'd just seen him do about the most moving job I've ever seen in the theatre.

So that's James Stewart. No school actor he. Instinctual. He started out being good and learned his craft and became great.

The films got him a year or so later but they didn't know what they had at first. He kept delivering with what they gave him though, making small waves, and the rest is history.

HENRY FONDA
New York City

Preface

This book, begun in June 1967 and completed in July 1968, has taught us to respect the perception and kindness of many people. We are grateful to Kenneth G. Lawrence, Los Angeles, California, for contributing the still photo from Mr. Stewart's first film, *Murder Man,* when all other sources proved unsuccessful; Steve Souttar, Columbia, Missouri; Richard Ytell, Commonwealth Theaters, Inc.; Roseann Gargotta and Judi White for their bibliographical and typing assistance; Judy B. Bond, faithful friend and secretary for typing the final manuscript; Leonard Maltin, editor of *Film Fan Monthly,* for his able assistance with the research; and Nancy Jones and Judy McClure for their practical help, not the least of which included keeping the children quiet while their Daddies labored.

KEN D. JONES
ARTHUR F. MCCLURE
ALFRED E. TWOMEY

Warrensburg, Missouri

The Films
of
James Stewart

Long-winded writers I abhor,
   and glib, prolific chatters;
give me the ones who tear and gnaw
   their hair and pens to tatters:
who find their writing such a chore
   they only write what matters.

               —from *Grooks*
                by Piet Hein

James Stewart:
The Sober Enthusiast

On May 20, 1968, James Stewart became 60 years of age. It is a difficult thing to imagine Jimmy Stewart, the embodiment of plodding but triumphant virtue, as being anything but young. But if *he* is 60, then we *all* must be a bit older. Audiences remember Stewart's early career as a somewhat baffled and fumbling but decent young man. This was during the "Golden days of Hollywood" in the late 1930s and early 1940s when, according to John Clellon Holmes:

> One's boyhood experience of the Depression may center around a Hooverville or a house in the suburbs, but one's fantasies of those years are likely to inhabit that carefree world, as shiny and shallow as patent leather, where Fred Astaire and Ginger Rogers denied all shabiness and anxiety for a few hypnotic hours.

And there was Jimmy Stewart.

During the 33 years that have elapsed between *Murder Man,* his first feature film made in 1935 and *Firecreek,* distributed in 1968, Stewart has enjoyed a career that unlike those of many stars of long duration has at no time really taken a downward turn.

There is a fitting but paradoxical tribute paid to him by his fans— his acting is so natural that he is seldom thought of as an actor. For more than one generation of moviegoers, his likeableness, his hesitant drawl, and his awkward manner have made him the personification of the slow and courageous winner over extreme odds. As Pete Martin once wrote:

> The Stewart the public sees is the Average Man, not the Man of Distinction. Instinctively, audiences think of the screen Stewart as a product of a small American town and of God-fearing parents endowed with a saving sense of humor. It is impossible to think of the screen Stewart as an egotist or a braggart.

James Maitland Stewart grew up in Indiana, Pennsylvania, the son of Alexander Maitland and Elizabeth Ruth Jackson Stewart.

The Stewart family had been in the hardware business there since 1853 and young James liked nothing better than to visit the store. As a child he was thin, wore glasses, and his pet ambition was to be a magician. He also dabbled in chemistry, radio, and parlor tricks. While a member of a local Boy Scout troop he wrote, produced and acted in his first play, which was about the World War then going on. He recruited his two younger sisters for parts in the production.

Acting in school plays at Model School, adjunct of the state teachers' college, and at Mercersburg Academy, from which he was graduated in 1928, Stewart was an accordion player of some accomplishment when he entered Princeton. He was uncertain as to what career he wanted to follow, but he started out with a major in civil engineering, later switched to steam engineering. He finally took up the study of architecture and earned his B. S. in 1932. When not at his studies he was at his accordion or rehearsing for a Triangle Club play and in the fall of 1931 he was a cheerleader. During vacations he and his friend Bill Neff barnstormed in their home territory with an act that combined accordion music with magic.

After graduation Stewart made his stage debut as the chauffeur in *Goodbye Again* in West Falmouth, Massachusetts, where his friend Josh Logan ran the summer theatre with a group called The University Players. His plan was to return to graduate school in the fall. Jobs were scarce, however, during those Depression years, and Stewart was glad to play the accordion for guests at the Old Silver Black Tea Room, also run by Logan. Stewart played bit parts in *Whistling In the Dark* and in the tryout of *Goodbye Again*. His first New York play was the short-lived *Carrie Nation,* which opened at the Biltmore Theatre in October 1932, in which he played the role of Constable Gano. He subsequently was added to the cast of *Goodbye Again,* which began its Broadway run in the fall of 1932. He repeated his role as the chauffeur. The *New York Sun* critic said of his performance, "It seems apropos to say a few words about James Stewart, a player in this mad piece, who is on the stage for exactly three minutes and speaks no more than eight lines. Yet before this gentleman exits he makes a definite impression on audiences because he makes them laugh so hard."

In 1933 Stewart was given the position as stage manager for the Boston run of Jane Cowl's production of *Camille.* In October 1933, Blanche Yurka hired him to stage-manage *Spring in Autumn,* in which he played Jack Breenan. When it folded producer Arthur Beckhard found room for Stewart in his New York office, then for a part as Johnny Chadwick in *All Good Americans,* which opened in December 1933.

During these years in New York Stewart and some of his friends, including Henry Fonda, Burgess Meredith, Myron McCormick, Josh Logan, Charles Arnt, and others organized what they called the "Thursday Night Beer Club." They often had such guests as Margaret Sullavan, whom Stewart had dated when she visited Princeton, Helen Hayes, Katharine Cornell, Kent Smith, Benny Goodman, and Mildred Natwick.

Stewart's first important Broadway role was as the idealistic Sgt. O'Hara in Sidney Kingsley's *Yellow Jack*, which opened at the Martin Beck Theater, March 6, 1934, and had a respectable run. His performance pleased the critics. Stewart later appeared as Teddy Parrish in *Divided by Three*, which opened at the Ethel Barrymore Theater, October 2, 1934; as Ed Olsen in *Page Miss Glory*, which opened at the Mansfield, November 27, 1934; and as Carl in *A Journey by Night*, which opened at the Schubert, April 16, 1935. After 1935, the only other stage appearance he has made during his career was in 1947 when he succeeded Frank Fay as Elwood P. Dowd in *Harvey*, a role he later repeated in the film version.

Stewart spent a summer working at the Locust Valley Theater on Long Island and it was during this period that he gained his first film experience. It was a long forgotten two-reel comedy made by Warner Brothers in a Long Island studio. He seemed to be intrigued more by the good pay than by the prospect of a screen career. In 1935, however, after a good year in several plays, he took a screen test at Fox. It was, he said, "one of those watch-the-horses-run affairs —you gravely turn your head from one side to the other, and assume that you're observing something intently."

Nothing came of it, but his next test for Billy Grady, the Metro-Goldwyn-Mayer talent scout, got him a contract. In the summer of 1935 Stewart arrived by train in Hollywood and established bachelor quarters with Henry Fonda, one of his former New York roommates. His first screen role was as the police reporter "Shorty" in *Murder Man*, which starred Spencer Tracy. Stewart was billed ninth and was not really impressive in a small part.

Subsequent pictures were much more successful in the pre-World War II years and included *Wife Versus Secretary* (MGM, 1936); *Next Time We Love* (Universal, 1936); opposite Margaret Sullavan, with whom he had appeared in stage productions; and *Seventh Heaven* (20th Century-Fox, 1937). In the following year he did *Shopworn Angel* for MGM, *Vivacious Lady* for RKO and *You Can't Take It With You* for Columbia. The latter was an outstanding comedy success, adjudged the best film of the year for 1938 by the Academy Awards. In a fast-paced Western, *Destry Rides Again* (1939), Stewart shared honors with Marlene Dietrich. In 1940 he made *The Shop Around the Corner* and *The Mortal Storm*, co-starring in both with Margaret Sullavan.

Mr. Smith Goes To Washington was one of the most talked-about pictures of 1939. Stewart's acting in the role of Mr. Smith won for him the New York Critics' Award for the Best Male Performance of the year, and he was runner-up for first place in the Film Critics of America voting. The film, said *Theatre Arts,* was more fun than the Senate itself and "We like to remember the way his voice cracked when he got up to read his bill, and the way he dropped his hat when he met the senior Senator's daughter, and the way he whistled at the Senators when they turned their backs on him." The New York Film Critics' Award was presented by Mayor Fiorello La Guardia who, as a former Congressman, praised Stewart for the authenticity of his performance. Stewart's performance as Mr. Smith probably did more to set the Stewart Style in the eyes of the public than any other pre-war film.

As the reporter in *The Philadelphia Story,* James Stewart did what many still think was perhaps his finest acting job. It was, said *The New York Times,* a "brilliant performance," and almost all critics concurred in this judgment. Stewart was a strong candidate for an Academy Award in 1939 for his role as Mr. Smith, but he lost in the balloting. His role in *The Philadelphia Story,* however, was unbeatable and he won his Oscar for that role in 1940.

In early 1941 Stewart was still underweight at 140 pounds and deferred by the draft board because of it. MGM was relieved, but by stuffing himself with fattening foods he was finally accepted on March 21, nearly a year before Pearl Harbor. He thereby became the first motion picture star to enlist. An experienced aviator with a plane of his own, Stewart was assigned to the Air Corps. According to news reports he took a pay cut of $11,979 monthly—the difference between his Army remuneration of $21 monthly as a private and his reported Hollywood income of $12,000 for the same period. Although he was eligible for release from the Army because of age he elected to remain in the service. Stewart deeply resented any attempts to coddle and surround him with publicity during his first weeks in service and used what influence he did have to request that he be treated like everyone else.

Winning his wings in August 1942, at Moffet Field, California, Stewart instructed bombardier cadets until November 1943, when he went to Europe as a pilot with an Eighth Air Force bomber squadron. He flew 25 missions over enemy territory, some of them as command pilot of a B-24 bomber wing with the 445th Bombardment Group. He led his outfit in a bomber named "Nine Yanks and a Jerk." He returned to the United States in September 1945 with the rank of Colonel and was decorated with the Air Medal and the Distinguished Flying Cross with Oak Leaf Cluster, the Croix de Guerre with Palm, and seven battle stars. Stewart remained active in the Air Force Reserve, and finally attained the rank of Brigadier General in July 1959 after Senator Margaret Chase Smith dropped her widely publicized opposition.

For Stewart, *It's a Wonderful Life* in 1946 was more than just another movie. It was the test, which others failed, of whether he still had the knack of playing before the cameras, after more than four years of military duty. In this film Stewart was also fortunate to have had Frank Capra as his producer-director. Before accepting the starring role in the film, however, Stewart outlined one condition, which was written into his contract. At his insistence, it was specified that nowhere in all the publicity and advertising issued by the producers of the film was there to be any "mention or cause to be mentioned the part taken by his participation as an officer in the U.S. Army."

It's a Wonderful Life was the first production for Liberty Films, a small movie company owned mostly by Capra, William Wyler and George Stevens. Stewart got off to a good postwar start with this role. As any movie buff knows, nearly all the best Frank Capra movies had the same hero. Generally played by Gary Cooper or Stewart, they were honest, likeable and naive young men who get played for suckers by the Philistines of this world. The hero of *It's a Wonderful Life* is George Bailey, who runs a small building-and-loan company in upstate New York. All his life George yearns to get out of Bedford Falls and travel to far-off places, but circumstances and responsibility to others always keep him tethered. At 39, he is poor, married and the father of four when his bank suddenly faces ruin and George himself faces jail. Discouraged and convinced that his life has been a complete failure, he decides to commit suicide. Then a guardian angel appears, shows George what would have happened to his town and to the people he loves if he had never been born. He is sufficiently appalled by what he sees to realize he has done considerable good with his life. This was certainly Stewart's kind of role.

Capra's $2.7 million production was a masterful edifice of comedy and sentiment, and Stewart was excellent in one of the longest movie roles on record up to that time. His first postwar role seemed to enhance a new-found maturity as an actor, and he was rewarded with his third Academy Award nomination.

The first postwar movies he made thus more or less carried on the stereotype that he had created before the war—the role described by Pete Martin as "the decent, homey Mr. Smith."

Starting in the late 1940s, however, the screen Stewart kept both his drawling speech and hesitant manner, but he displayed them in new settings where they lost some of the juvenile bumbling and gained variety. In 1948, when he made *Call Northside 777*, in which in which he played a hard-boiled reporter, he began to shift away from the "Stewart norm." Further evidence of this trend was seen in Alfred Hitchcock's *Rope*, in which Stewart played the young murderers' suspicious former headmaster, and in *Malaya* in 1950, in which he portrayed a patriotic World War II smuggler of Far Eastern rubber.

When in 1950 he played Elwood P. Dowd, the drunk with an invisible giant rabbit for his companion, in a screen version of *Harvey*, Stewart emphasized Dowd's pixilation more than his inebriation. Although many critics felt that Stewart was bending the dipsomaniac to the old Stewart formula, their reaction was in general, favorable. He was also nominated for an Oscar for the fourth time.

The filming of *Winchester '73* in 1950 witnessed the genesis of Stewart, the raw frontiersman. With this type of characterization, Stewart fell in love with an Apache maiden in *Broken Arrow* (1950), led pioneers to Oregon in *Bend of the River* (1952), hunted down an outlaw in *Naked Spur* (1953), rooted out a villain selling guns to Apaches in *The Man from Laramie* (1955), fought rawhide outlaws who robbed his herd in *The Far Country* (1955), and foiled railroad payroll robbers in *Night Passage* (1957). Although some reviewers found it difficult to adjust to the sight of Stewart riding the range with a day's growth of beard, the adult westerns of the 1950s opened up for him an entirely new vein of critical praise.

The Stratton Story in 1949 began another line of portrayal that formed a pattern: the historic and popular hero, or potential hero. While *Carbine Williams,* filmed in 1952—a biography of Marsh Williams, the chain gang prisoner who invented the 30-caliber M-1 carbine rifle—was not received enthusiastically, *The Glenn Miller Story* was a great critical and popular success when released in 1954 and reissued in 1960. Stewart's percentage of the profits from this film alone made him a very wealthy man.

As Charles A. Lindbergh, a role he had wanted for years, in *The Spirit of St. Louis* in 1957, he drew critical attention to the ease with he transformed himself into the young flyer, but the movie itself was a disappointment at the box office. He also played heroic types in *Strategic Air Command* in 1955 and *The F.B.I. Story* in 1959. In several of these biographical and semidocumentary films, June Allyson played opposite Stewart, who likes to work regularly with the same actors and directors because of the time and trouble saved by customary cooperation and understanding.

Perhaps the most offbeat Stewart role in the 1950s was a minor part that he himself requested: the clown with the mysterious past who never takes the smiling paint off his sad face in Cecil B. DeMille's 1952 production of *The Greatest Show on Earth*. The starring roles in three suspense films made by Alfred Hitchcock during the 1950s were also among his credits: *Rear Window* (1954), *The*

Man Who Knew Too Much (1956), and *Vertigo* (1958). All were very popular with audiences.

Other movies in which Stewart appeared through 1960 were *On Our Merry Way* (1948), *You Gotta Stay Happy* (1948), *The Jackpot* (1950), *No Highway in the Sky* (1951), *Thunder Bay* (1953), *Bell, Book and Candle* (1958), and *The Mountain Road* (1960). For his role as the defense lawyer in the trial of an Army officer in *Anatomy of a Murder* (1959) he won awards from the Venice Film Festival, the New York Film Critics, the annual *Film Daily* poll of writers, and was nominated for his fifth Academy Award.

Since 1960 Stewart has increasingly returned to westerns with roles in *Two Rode Together* (1961), *The Man Who Shot Liberty Valance* (1962), *How the West Was Won* (1962), *Cheyenne Autumn* (1963), *Shenandoah* (1965), *The Rare Breed* (1967), *Firecreek* (1968) and *Bandolero!* (1968). In 1961 Stewart narrated *X-15,* the semi-documentary story of the Air Force's experimental supersonic plane. He has starred in three comedies, *Mr. Hobbs Takes a Vacation* (1962), *Take Her, She's Mine* (1963), and *Dear Brigitte* (1965). He also had an interesting role as a broken-down pilot in *Flight of the Phoenix* (1966).

In October 1962 he played ballplayer Slim Conway in *Flashing Spikes* on ABC television's *Alcoa Presents*. In recent years he has appeared on some top television panel and variety shows, including several guest appearances on the *Dean Martin Show* in 1968.

The end of the 1940s marked a turning point not only for James Stewart as an actor but also as a businessman. He worked out a payment plan, later used by many other high-priced stars, whereby he would receive a percentage of net profits instead of a flat $250,000 salary. This new participation arrangement made him one of Hollywood's highest-paid actors as well as one of its most shrewd businessmen. Stewart's investments in recent years are widely varied, and include ranching.

In Stewart's private life, he has carefully avoided the usual Hollywood specifications for stars. His homespun looks, and his famous cornflakes-and-syrup drawl have never ranked him as one of the great screen lovers or ten handsomest men. But he has never once been involved in any Hollywood scandal or gossip, and has assumed instead a quiet but tasteful nearly universal fame.

James Stewart and Gloria Hatrick McLean were married on August 9, 1949. Stewart was 41 years of age when he ended Hollywood's most famous bachelorhood. The Stewarts live in a large, vine-covered house in Beverly Hills. There are four children: two boys, Ronald and Michael, by Mrs. Stewart's previous marriage, and twin girls, Judy and Kelly, born on May 7, 1951. Stewart has been described as a good companion to his children, but a strict disciplinarian. He is methodical to the point of being meticulous about his modest wardrobe, his tool room, his photographic equipment, as well as the household in general.

Stewart and his wife do little entertaining, but instead enjoy golfing, fishing, and picnicking with their children. Stewart holds a commercial pilot's license and owns his own aircraft. After an interview in which Stewart talked about the Strategic Air Command, Richard Dyer MacCann noted in the *Christian Science Monitor* that "There is a sober enthusiasm . . . about his devotion to air power which makes you forget entirely that this is Jimmy Stewart, everybody's favorite hometown boy in the movies."

Six feet, three and one-half inches tall, James Stewart weighs approximately 167 pounds and has graying brown hair and gray eyes. Louella Parsons once called him "the most nearly normal of all Hollywood Stars." He is a worrier, nervous when he is not working and nervous during previews of his films. A hard worker accustomed to accepting the discipline of his craft, he is willing to go over and over a scene until it is right.

Stewart is an adviser to Princeton University's Theatre in Residence, the first professional repertory company sponsored by an American university; a member of the executive board of the Los Angeles council, Boy Scouts of America; a member of the board of directors of the Air Force Association. He and his family attend the Beverly Hills Community Presbyterian Church. In 1959 he was elected to the Princeton University board of trustees, with much less publicity than he received from his promotion to Brigadier General.

In February 1968, at the 30th annual awards banquet of Delta Kappa Alpha cinema fraternity chapter at the University of Southern California, Mervyn LeRoy, Mae West, and Stewart were all honored for their contributions to films. Film clips were presented from three of Stewart's films—*Philadelphia Story, Harvey,* and *On Our Merry Way.* In addition, a clip was shown from an old Ed Sullivan show, which showed Stewart recreating his first professional job, a Josh Logan song from a Princeton Triangle show.

In the spring of 1968, Stewart toured military bases during his last two weeks of active duty before retiring from the Air Force Reserve. He spoke to the members of the 445th military airlift wing, his old World War II organization, who were recalled to active duty at Dobbins A.F.B. in Marietta, Ga. Upon his retirement, after 27 years of service, he received the Distinguished Service Medal from the Air Force, only the second time that the honor had been bestowed on a Reserve officer. The citation read in part that "the singularly distinctive accomplishments of General Stewart culminate a long and distinguished career in the service of his country and reflect the highest credit upon himself and the U.S. Air Force."

At the 1960 Academy Awards show on April 17, 1961, it was Stewart's sad duty to announce that Gary Cooper was to receive a special award for his contributions to motion pictures. Stewart's voice choked with emotion, as his old friend lay seriously ill at the time. Cooper, at whose home Stewart had met his future wife years before, died less than a month later. Clark Gable had passed away only a few months before that.

Stewart, along with Cary Grant and a precious few others, is one of the few male stars of his generation left. In June 1968 he went to Dallas for the world premier of *Bandolero!* and stated in his typically honest fashion in a *Variety* interview that personal appearances should be considered by actors "as part of your job . . . It gets a picture started . . . It shouldn't be just hard core promotion. It should have civic overtones and you just participate in it . . ." In Stewart's opinion he enjoys "getting out to different parts of the country and meeting people who show a genuine interest in pictures and picture people. Some people will come up to you and say 'I don't know whether this means anything to you but our whole family saw your last picture and we liked you in it.' "

Stewart answered this with two questions, "Does it mean anything? Why, what the hell else is there?"

John Ford once said of Stewart, "People just seem to like him." His image on the screen and in real life remains that of the gentle, relaxed and hesitant man. And yet for all of his experience, the impression of slight nervousness is still there. It is undoubtedly this expression of the man's humility that audiences can still identify with in a sometimes cruel and cynical world. And those same audiences are grateful that the years have made little difference in the quality of the man who is one of the few remaining Hollywood immortals.

Murder Man

DISTRIBUTOR: M-G-M
RUNNING TIME: 70 minutes
CAST: Spencer Tracy, Virginia Bruce, Lionel Atwill, Harvey Stephens, Robert Barrat, James Stewart, William Collier, Sr., Bobby Watson, William Demarest, John Sheehan, Lucien Littlefield, George Chandler, Fuzzy Knight, Louise Henry, Robert Warwick, Joe Irving, Ralph Bushman
PRODUCER: Harry Rapf
DIRECTOR: Tim Whelan
AUTHORS: Tim Whelan, Guy Bolton
SCREEN PLAY: Tim Whelan, John C. Higgins
CAMERAMAN: Lester White
EDITOR: James E. Newcomb
REVIEWED: 7–9–35
RELEASED: 7–9–35

With Spencer Tracy (far right) in *Murder Man*

SYNOPSIS:

Steve Grey (Spencer Tracy) portrays a dashing newspaper reporter. As a newspaperman, he is smart and disarming enough to be a step ahead of the police department in solving crimes. This is true even though he is described by his editor as a "crazy, cynical, drunken bum." Grey usually passes the night by either sleeping on a Merry-go-round or riding up and down in an elevator. Mary Shannon (Virginia Bruce) another reporter continually tries to reform him.

Henry Mander (Harvey Stephens) is a ruthless financier and along with a partner victimizes Grey's father, Pop, (William Collier, Sr.) and causes the suicide of Grey's errant wife.

Grey plans the perfect crime and kills Mander's partner and so twists reports that Mander is arrested and convicted of the murder. In a death house interview with Mander, Grey gloats over his revenge until his sense of honor and decency causes him to confess that through desire for one grand headline story and revenge he is the killer. Stewart played "Shorty," a fledgling police reporter, and was billed ninth.

New York Herald Tribune, July 27, 1935

"There are several good performances in the minor roles. That admirable stage juvenile, James Stewart, who was so fine in *Yellow Jack,* is wasted in a bit that he handles with characteristically engaging skill."

Rose Marie

Rose Marie

DISTRIBUTOR: M-G-M
RUNNING TIME: 110 minutes
CAST: Jeanette MacDonald, Nelson Eddy, Reginald Owen, Allan Jones, James Stewart, Alan Mowbray, Gilda Gray, George Regas, Robert Greig, Una O'Connor, Lucien Littlefield, David Niven, Herman Bing
PRODUCER: Hunt Stromberg
DIRECTOR: W. S. Van Dyke
AUTHORS: Otto A. Harbach, Oscar Hammerstein, II
SCREEN PLAY: Frances Goodrich, Albert Hackett, Alice Duer Miller
MUSIC: Rudolf Friml, Herbert Stothar
ADDITIONAL LYRICS: Gus Kahn
CAMERAMAN: William Daniels
EDITOR: Blanche Sewell
REVIEWED: 1-13-36
RELEASED: 1-13-36

SYNOPSIS:

Marie de Flor (Jeanette MacDonald) is a temperamental opera singer who is human only to her brother, John (Stewart). John has escaped from prison and has killed the Royal Northwest mounted policeman in pursuit of him.

With George Regas, Nelson Eddy in *Rose Marie*

28 The Films of James Stewart

Robert Greig, Gilda Gray, Nelson Eddy in *Rose Marie*

Marie is at the height of a triumph in Montreal, but hearing that her brother is hiding out in the lake country she rushes off to find him. She is robbed and deserted by her guide and attempts to match her artistic talents with a honky tonky dance hall girl. She meets and is befriended by Sergeant Bruce (Nelson Eddy). They fall in love but Sergeant Bruce still realizes his duty and captures her brother.

She returns to the Opera, but collapses and is returned to the Northland to recuperate. She reunites with Sergeant Bruce.

New York Herald Tribune, February 1, 1936

"There is a good performance by James Stewart, the hero of the current picture at the Radio City Music Hall, in the role of Miss MacDonald's runaway brother."

Next Time We Love

DISTRIBUTOR: Universal
RUNNING TIME: 87 minutes
CAST: Margaret Sullavan, James Stewart, Ray Milland, Grant Mitch-

ell, Robert McWade, Anna Demetrio, Ronnie Cosbey, Florence Roberts, Christian Rub, Charles Fallon, Nat Carr, Gottlieb Huber
PRODUCER: Paul Kohner
DIRECTOR: Edward H. Griffith
AUTHOR: Ursula Parrott
SCREEN PLAY: Melville Baker
CAMERAMAN: Joseph Valentine
EDITOR: Ted Kent
REVIEWED: 1-31-36
RELEASED: 1-27-36

SYNOPSIS:

The storyline of this film is an investigation of the problem of marriage vs. career.

Cicely Tyler (Margaret Sullavan) is excited about her newspaper reporter husband Christopher Tyler (Stewart) as well as her career as an actress. When Christopher receives his first foreign assignment in Rome, Cicely refuses to accompany him. Later she confides to the best friend, Tommy Abbott (Ray Milland) that she refuses to accompany her husband because she is going to have a baby and does not want to be a bother. There follows a series of separations caused

With Anna Demetrio, Margaret Sullavan in *Next Time We Love*

With Margaret Sullavan in *Next Time We Love*

With Margaret Sullavan in *Next Time We Love*

by Cicely's desire to remain at home and become a celebrity on Broadway and Christopher's urge to rove about Rome, Moscow and China with his typewriter.

New York Times, January 31, 1936

"James Stewart, known to playgoers for his work in *Yellow Jack, Divided by Three* and *Page Miss Glory,* promises in this his first picture to reach New York to be a welcome addition to the roster of Hollywood's leading men."

Time, February 10, 1936

"The chief significance of *Next Time We Love* in the progress of the cinema industry is likely to reside in the presence in its cast of James Stewart. . . . He disregards a long established cinema convention for such roles, ably introduces to Hollywood the character of a newspaper man who is neither drunkard, lecher nor buffoon."

Wife Versus Secretary

DISTRIBUTOR: M-G-M
RUNNING TIME: 88 minutes
CAST: Clark Gable, Jean Harlow, Myrna Loy, May Robson, George Barbier, James Stewart, Hobart Cavanaugh, Tom Dugan, Gilbert Emery
PRODUCER: Hunt Stromberg
DIRECTOR: Clarence Brown
AUTHOR: Faith Baldwin
SCREEN PLAY: Norman Krasna, Alice Duer Miller, John Lee Mahin
CAMERAMAN: Ray June
EDITOR: Frank E. Hull
REVIEWED: 2–19–36
RELEASED: 2–28–36

SYNOPSIS:

Magazine publisher Van Sanford (Clark Gable) is very much in love with his wife Linda (Myrna Loy). His job makes it necessary that he have his secretary, Whitney (Jean Harlow), on call at all times. The intimate association, always strictly business, presents a problem when Van's mother Mimi (May Robson) plants the first seed of suspicion in Linda's mind. Whitney and her boy friend, Dave (Stewart) argue and stop seeing each other when she refuses to leave her job to marry him.

Van takes a business trip to Havana and is later joined by Whitney who has some important information regarding the deal. Linda was disillusioned when Van explained he could not take her along and

With Jean Harlow in *Wife Vs. Secretary*

Clark Gable with Jean Harlow in *Wife Vs. Secretary*

Small Town Girl

then fears the worse when Whitney is missing from the office. She telephones Van at his hotel and when Whitney answers she is convinced they are having an affair and separates from Van.

Linda is confronted by Whitney in the stateroom of her Europe-bound boat. Whitney tells Linda there has never been anything between her and Van, but there could be if she leaves. Linda realizes she's been foolish and goes back to Van and Whitney realizes a marriage is more important than a career and reconciles with Dave.

New York Herald Tribune
"James Stewart is of help as the secretary's rather badly treated fiance."

Small Town Girl

DISTRIBUTOR: M-G-M
RUNNING TIME: 90 minutes
CAST: Janet Gaynor, Robert Taylor, Binnie Barnes, Lewis Stone, Andy Devine, Elizabeth Patterson, Frank Craven, James Stewart, Douglas Fowley, Isabel Jewell, Charley Grapewin, Nella Walker, Robert Greig, Edgar Kennedy, Willie Fung
PRODUCER: Hunt Stromberg
DIRECTOR: William A. Wellman
AUTHOR: Ben Ames Williams
SCREEN PLAY: John Lee Mahin, Edith Fitzgerald
ART DIRECTOR: Cedric Gibbons
CAMERAMAN: Charles Rosher
EDITOR: Blanche Sewell
REVIEWED: 4-2-36
RELEASED: 4-10-36

SYNOPSIS:

Kay Brannan (Janet Gaynor) is bored in the small town of Carvel, Massachusetts. She watches the gay crowds every Saturday in Autumn on their way to football games. On one return trip Dr. Bob Dakin (Robert Taylor) asks her for directions then persuades her to go along to guide him. There is a wild nightclub party and the next morning he awakens from an alcoholic haze to learn they are married.

Bob is actually engaged to Priscilla (Binnie Barnes), who doesn't feel the marriage should interfere with their romance. Bob is also bitter about the marriage but for appearance's sake decides to let the marriage stand for six months. He renews his association with Priscilla. One of Bob's patients takes a turn for the worse and Kay goes to Priscilla's apartment and drags her husband out to complete an

With Janet Gaynor in *Small Town Girl*

operation. She then goes back to Carvel.

She is reunited with her small town boy friend, Elmer (Stewart) and learns Bob is bound for Reno and divorce. Bob finally realizes whom he loves, comes back to Carvel and takes Kay back to Boston to make a go of their marriage.

New York Times, April 11, 1936
". . . James Stewart and an anonymous brat cooperated handsomely as living portraits from a small town family's album."

Speed

DISTRIBUTOR: M-G-M
RUNNING TIME: 65 minutes
CAST: James Stewart, Una Merkel, Ted Healy, Wendy Barrie, Weldon Heyburn, Ralph Morgan, Patricia Wilder
PRODUCER: Lucien Hubbard
DIRECTOR: Edwin L. Marin
AUTHORS: Milton Krims, Larry Bachman

With Ted Healy in *Speed*

With Una Merkel, Weldon Heyburn in *Speed*

SCREEN PLAY: Michael Fessier
CAMERAMAN: Lester White
EDITOR: Harry Poppe
REVIEWED: 4-29-36
RELEASED: 5-8-36

SYNOPSIS:

Terry Martin (Stewart) is a young test driver who is specializing in the development of a new high-speed carburetor. He is also interested in the owner's niece June Mitchell (Wendy Barrie). She also is the object of engineer Frank Lawson's (Weldon Heyburn) attentions. When Terry has trouble perfecting his invention, Lawson feels he can provide a solution. Terry resents this but allows him to assist thanks to Jane's urging.

They try the new carburetor on the Indianapolis Speedway and Terry's car crashes, injuring the driver, Gadget (Ted Healy). Terry is overcome by fumes and is saved by Frank. They return to the factory and perfect the carburetor. In a race against time the invention is proved practical and Terry is promoted and wins Jane's hand.

New York Times, May 16, 1936
"Mr. Stewart, Miss Barrie and the rest perform as pleasantly as possible."

The Gorgeous Hussy

DISTRIBUTOR: M-G-M
RUNNING TIME: 102 minutes
CAST: Joan Crawford, Robert Taylor, Lionel Barrymore, Franchot Tone, Melvyn Douglas, James Stewart, Alison Skipworth, Louis Calhern, Beulah Bondi, Melville Cooper, Edith Atwater, Sidney Toler, Gene Lockhart, Pheobe Foster, Clara Blandick, Frank Conroy, Nydia Westman, Willard Robertson, Charles Trowbridge, Greta Meyer, Snowflake
PRODUCER: Joseph Mankiewicz
DIRECTOR: Clarence Brown
AUTHOR: Samuel Hopkins Adams
SCREEN PLAY: Ainsworth Morgan, Stephen Morehouse Avery
MUSICAL SCORES: Herbert Stothart
DANCE STAGED BY: Val Raset
CAMERAMAN: George Folsey
ART DIRECTOR: Cedric Gibbons
EDITOR: Blanche Sewell
REVIEWED: 9-1-36
RELEASED: 8-28-36

Born To Dance

SYNOPSIS:

This is the story of an inn-keeper's daughter who married a sailor and then a Secretary of War, loves a famous Virginia Senator, and was the counsellor of the President of the United States.

Washington is in the midst of a presidential election with Andrew Jackson (Lionel Barrymore) opposing John C. Calhoun (Frank Conroy). Peggy Eaton (Joan Crawford) is close to Jackson's heart. She is in love with Senator John Randolph (Melvyn Douglas), but he will not marry her as he feels he is too old. She marries "Bow" Timberlake (Robert Taylor) a young sailor who is soon killed in a sea battle.

Andrew Jackson's wife, Rachel (Beulah Bondi) is his strongest support but she dies as a result of a vicious tongue lashing. Andrew Jackson can not fulfill his presidential duties until Peggy is by his side. Jackson and Senator Randolph have bitter political differences and Randolph finally wants to marry Peggy but she turns him down to be at the side of Jackson.

She marries John Eaton (Franchot Tone), Secretary of War, but this fails to halt gossip aimed in her direction. Jackson dismisses his entire cabinet to avenge her name. Stewart played one of Peggy Eaton's many admirers.

New York Herald Tribune, September 5, 1936
"James Stewart is fine as 'Rowdy' Dow."

Born To Dance

DISTRIBUTOR: M-G-M
RUNNING TIME: 108 minutes
CAST: Eleanor Powell, James Stewart, Virginia Bruce, Una Merkel, Sid Silvers, Francis Langford, Raymond Walburn, Alan Dinehart, Buddy Ebsen, William Mandel, Joe Mandel, Juanita Quigley, Georges and Jalja, Reginald Gardiner, J. Marshall Smith, L. Dwight Snyder, Jay Johnson, Del Porter
ASST. PRODUCER: Jack Cummings
DIRECTOR: Roy Del Ruth
AUTHOR: Jack McGowan, Sid Silvers, B. G. DeSylva
SCREEN PLAY: Jack McGowan, Sid Silvers
MUSIC AND LYRICS: Cole Porter
MUSICAL DIRECTOR: Alfred Newman
MUSICAL ARRANGEMENTS: Roger Edens
DANCES: Dave Gould
CAMERAMAN: Ray June
EDITOR: Blanche Sewell
REVIEWED: 11-21-36
RELEASED: 11-27-36

With Buddy Ebsen, Frances Langford, Eleanor Powell, Sid Silvers, Una Merkel, in *Born to Dance*

With Sid Silvers, Raymond Walburn, Buddy Ebsen in *Born To Dance*

After the Thin Man

SYNOPSIS:

Ted Barker (Stewart) is a bashful Navy non-commissioned officer. He meets dancer Nora Paige (Eleanor Powell) in a Lonely Hearts Club and they fall in love.

Producer McKay (Alan Dinehart) for publicity purposes fakes a romance between his temperamental star Lucy James (Virginia Bruce) and Ted. The gag backfires for McKay and Lucy as Nora steps into her spot in the show. This occurs when Lucy walks out when Ted does some legitimate double-crossing to make Nora the reigning singing and dancing sensation of Broadway.

New York Times, December 5, 1936

"There is a story which very probably doesn't amount to much. It amounts to just enough to serve to introduce Jimmy Stewart as a lank, amiable guy in a quartermaster's uniform whose singing and dancing will (fortunately) never win him a song-and-dance-man classification."

" . . . Even Mr. Stewart takes an embarrassed turn at a chorus or so."

After the Thin Man

DISTRIBUTOR: M-G-M
RUNNING TIME: 110 minutes
CAST: William Powell, Myrna Loy, James Stewart, Elissa Landi, Joseph Calleia, Jessie Ralph, Alan Marshall, Teddy Hart, Sam Levene, Dorothy McNulty, William Law, George Zucco, Paul Fix
PRODUCER: Hunt Stromberg
DIRECTOR: W. S. Van Dyke
AUTHOR: Dashiell Hammett
SCREEN PLAY: Francis Goodrich, Albert Hackett
MUSICAL SCORE: Herbert Stothart, Edward Ward
MUSIC AND LYRICS: Nacio Herb Brown, Arthur Freed, Walter Donaldson, Bob Wright, Chet Forrest
CAMERAMAN: Oliver T. Marsh
EDITOR: Robert J. Kern
REVIEWED: 12-7-36
RELEASED: 12-25-36

SYNOPSIS:

Nick Charles (William Powell) and his wife Nora (Myrna Loy) come to San Francisco for their honeymoon. A party is already in progress when they arrive at their house. Aunt Katherine (Jessie Ralph) and the other in-laws soon get Nick involved in a family scandal.

With Elissa Landi in *After The Thin Man*

With Robert E. O'Connor in *After The Thin Man*

After the Thin Man 43

With Guy Usher, Myrna Loy, Robert E. O'Connor in *After The Thin Man*

Sister-in-law Selma's (Elissa Landi) philandering husband, Robert (Alan Marshall), has been murdered. Selma is jailed and Nick sets about to free her. His suspects are David (Stewart) who once wanted to marry her, night club entertainer Polly (Dorothy McNulty) with whom Robert had been playing around, racketeer Dancer (Joseph Calleia), tinhorn thug Casper (Teddy Hart) and Chinese Lum Kee (William Law).

Two more murders are committed. Casper is strangled and an unseen janitor shot. Nick, both aided and hampered by Nora, gathers all the suspects together and questions them certain that the guilty party will give himself away. His idea succeeds.

New York Herald Tribune, December 25, 1936
"The assisting players have been chosen wisely. There is James Stewart in a characterization that is as surprising as it is effective."

Seventh Heaven

DISTRIBUTOR: 20th Century-Fox
RUNNING TIME: 102 minutes
CAST: Simone Simon, James Stewart, Jean Hersholt, Gregory Ratoff, Gale Sondergaard, J. Edward Bromberg, John Qualen, Victor Kilian, Thomas Beck, Sig Rumann, Mady Christians, Rollo Lloyd, Rafaela Ottiano, Georges Renavent, Edward Keane, John Hamilton, Paul Porcasi, Will Stanton, Irving Bacon, Leonid Snegoff, Adrienne D'Ambricourt
ASSOCIATE PRODUCER: Raymond Griffith
DIRECTOR: Henry King
SCREEN PLAY: Melville Baker
CAMERAMAN: Merritt Gerstad
EDITOR: Barbara McLean
REVIEWED: 3-18-37
RELEASED: 3-26-37

SYNOPSIS:

A tale of two Paris tenement lovers who are torn asunder by war.

Chico (Stewart) is a sewer worker who denies God and love. Diane (Simone Simon) is tossed out of a brothel and whipped by her sister, Nana (Gale Sondergaard). Diane is saved by Chico and he takes her to his apartment. She immediately falls in love with him but he does not return her love. Father Chevillon (Jean Hersholt) in an effort to rid Chico of his Atheism has him promoted to street washer.

Chico and Diane eventually plan marriage, but war breaks out. Chico is recruited and they "marry in the sight of God." Every day for four years at eleven o'clock Diane knows that Chico is with her. With the coming of peace everyone tells Diane Chico is dead, but her faith tells her otherwise. Her faith is well founded as Chico, although blind, does indeed return to her.

New York Herald Tribune, March 26, 1937

". . . while James Stewart's Chico is little better than an odd caricature of the role, more comical than appealing."

"Mr. Stewart doesn't begin to make Chico come alive. He is an excellent actor, but he never makes you believe in his proudly shy and heroic sewerworker, living close to the chimney pots and averring that he is 'a very remarkable fellow.' He is just James Stewart, getting some laughs, at best, for his repulses of the adoring Diane."

In *Seventh Heaven*

With Simone Simon in *Seventh Heaven*

With Simone Simon in *Seventh Heaven*

The Films of James Stewart
The Last Gangster

DISTRIBUTOR: M-G-M
RUNNING TIME: 81 minutes
CAST: Edward G. Robinson, James Stewart, Rose Stradner, Lionel Stander, Douglas Scott, John Carradine, Sidney Blackmer, Grant Mitchell, Edward S. Brophy, Alan Baxter, Frank Conroy, Louise Beavers
DIRECTOR: Edward Ludwig
AUTHORS: William A. Wellman, Robert Carson
SCREEN PLAY: John Lee Hahin
CAMERAMAN: William Daniels
EDITOR: Ben Lewis
REVIEWED: 11-9-37
RELEASED: 11-2-37

SYNOPSIS:

Joe Krozac (Edward G. Robinson) a New York big shot is convicted of income tax evasion and sent to Alcatraz. His son is born to his wife, Talya (Rose Stradner), shortly afterward. She attempts to protect her son by divorcing the gangster and marries a newspaper man Paul North (Stewart).

With Douglas Scott in *The Last Gangster*

The Last Gangster

With Edward G. Robinson, Rose Stradner, Douglas Scott in *The Last Gangster*

With Rose Stradner, Sidney Blackmer in *The Last Gangster*

With Edward G. Robinson, Rose Stradner in *The Last Gangster*

On release from prison the gangster is met by former associates who torture him into revealing the whereabouts of his sudden fortune. His son is also kidnapped and abused as a final means of making him talk.

Joe restores the lad to his mother and contact with the boy changes his attitude. Joe is killed in a final duel with a vengeful rival, but kills the rival also to preserve the secret of the boy's identity. Federal men have already killed all the gangsters who knew it.

New York Herald Tribune, December 10, 1937
"Mr. Robinson has valuable support from the other players in the production. James Stewart is casually right as the nice fellow. . . ."

Navy Blue and Gold

DISTRIBUTOR: M-G-M
RUNNING TIME: 94 minutes
CAST: Robert Young, James Stewart, Florence Rice, Billie Burke, Lionel Barrymore, Tom Brown, Samuel S. Hinds, Paul Kelly, Barnett Parker, Frank Albertson, Minor Watson, Robert Middle-

Navy Blue and Gold 51

With Robert Young, Florence Rice in *Navy Blue and Gold*

mass, Philip Terry, Charles Waldron, Pat Flaherty, Stanley Morner (Dennis Morgan) Matt McNugh, Ted Pearson
PRODUCER: Sam Zimbalist
DIRECTOR: Sam Wood
AUTHOR: George Bruce
SCREEN PLAY: George Bruce
MONTAGE: John Hoffman
MUSICAL SCORE: Edward Ward
ART DIRECTOR: Cedric Gibbons
CAMERAMAN: John Seitz
EDITOR: Robert J. Kern
REVIEWED: 11-17-37
RELEASED: 11-19-37

SYNOPSIS:
This story traces the careers of three young men through Annapolis. Each of them looks at their opportunities from different angles, but each has the desire to play football.
In the second year Roger Ash (Robert Young) is demoted to substitute on the Varsity while his pals, "Truck" Cross (Stewart)

and Richard Gates, Jr. (Tom Brown) are stars and heroes to the student body.

In a classroom Cross listens to a lecture of how an officer brought disgrace to the Navy. Angered, he tells the true story and confesses the man was his father. He is suspended and his teammates go to the big game. Found guilty, he is granted leniency for his confession and is reinstated.

Ash is given his big chance in the game with Army and with the score tied 7–7 he shakes loose and follows the interference of Cross until crossing the goal line when he gives the ball to Cross, proving he is an officer and a gentleman. Cross is thereby given the right to ring the bell to an old football idol, Captain "Skinny" Davis (Lionel Barrymore).

New York Herald Tribune, December 24, 1937

". . . Moreover, it presents the engaging James Stewart in one of the best performances he has yet offered on the screen. If *Navy Blue and Gold* is not the most beguiling service-college picture yet filmed, it is not Mr. Stewart's fault."

"Mr. Stewart contributes the sort of portrayal that one would like

With Robert Young, Tom Brown, Lionel Barrymore in *Navy Blue and Gold*

Of Human Hearts

to see more frequently in the motion pictures—tour-de-force or no tour-de-force. Although he has been denied Robert Taylor's beauty and has been endowed with none of the strong, silent intensity of Gary Cooper, he breathes life into his character to hold a formulized theme to a strict pattern. It is due to his expert rendition of a rather preposterous part that a rather preposterous show becomes generally exciting."

Of Human Hearts

DISTRIBUTOR: Loew's, Inc.
RUNNING TIME: 100 minutes
CAST: Walter Huston, James Stewart, Gene Reynolds, Beulah Bondi, Guy Kibbee, Charles Coburn, John Carradine, Ann Rutherford, Leatrice Joy Gilbert, Charley Grapewin, Leona Roberts, Gene Lockhart, Clem Bevans, Arthur Aylesworth, Sterling Holloway, Charles Peck, Robert McWade, Minor Watson
PRODUCER: John W. Considine, Jr.

With Charles Coburn, Beulah Bondi, Ann Rutherford in *Of Human Hearts*

With John Carradine in *Of Human Hearts*

With John Miljan in *Of Human Hearts*

Of Human Hearts

With Walter Huston, Ann Rutherford in *Of Human Hearts*

DIRECTOR: Clarence Brown
AUTHOR: Honore Morrow (from "Benefits Forgot")
SCREEN PLAY: Bradbury Foote
CAMERAMAN: Clyde Devinna
EDITOR: Frank E. Hull
REVIEWED: 2-8-38
RELEASED: 2-11-38

SYNOPSIS:

The story concerns a righteous minister and his family in a small Ohio town during the period 1845 to 1862.

Ethan Wilkins (Walter Huston) is a stern uncomprising cleric teaching the scripture by text, precept, and brawn. His son, Jason Wilkins (Stewart) revolts against a life of hand-me-down clothes, unreasonable restraints and a code of behavior he can not abide. He rebels and runs away to medical school. His widowed mother, Mary Wilkins (Beulah Bondi) makes tireless sacrifices sending him to school and he later gains distinction as a surgeon in the Civil War.

After two years without a word from him she writes President

Lincoln regarding the whereabouts of Jason's grave, assuming him dead. President Lincoln (John Carradine) summons Jason from the front line, reprimands him, and sends him home on furlough.

New York Times, February 18, 1938

"And the other players, large and small, have in their turn become integral props in this re-creation of the frontier settlement. . . . James Stewart's and Master Reynolds's farm boy and all the others are flawlessly typical."

Movie Mirror, May, 1938

"There is no fault to find with production, direction or acting. The individual performance of each cast member—especially of Stewart, Miss Bondi, Huston and young Reynolds—is superlative."

Vivacious Lady

DISTRIBUTOR: RKO Radio
RUNNING TIME: 90 minutes

In *Vivacious Lady*

With Ginger Rogers, Frances Mercer in *Vivacious Lady*

CAST: Ginger Rogers, James Stewart, James Ellison, Beulah Bondi, Charles Coburn, Frances Mercer, Phyllis Kennedy, Franklin Pangborn, Grady Sutton, Jack Carson, Alec Craig, Willie Best
PRODUCER: George Stevens
DIRECTOR: George Stevens
AUTHOR: I. A. R. Wylie
SCREEN PLAY: P. J. Wolfson, Ernest Pagano
ART DIRECTOR: Van Nest Polglase
MUSICAL SCORE: Roy Webb
SONG: George Jessel, Jack Meskill, Ted Shapiro
CAMERAMAN: Robert de Grasse
EDITOR: Henry Berman
REVIEWED: 5-5-38
RELEASED: 5-13-38

SYNOPSIS:
Peter Morgan (Stewart), a young botany professor has lived his life under paternal domination. He goes to New York to spring a drunken cousin, Keith (James Ellison) from nightclubs. Instead he meets Francey (Ginger Rogers) a nightclub entertainer. They fall in love at first sight and marry within a span of an evening.

With Ginger Rogers in *Vivacious Lady*

Peter now has the problem of breaking the news to his family. His father, Mr. Morgan (Charles Coburn) is the University's president and he worships dignified tradition and respectability. His mother (Beulah Bondi) also is known for her convenient heart attacks. All of Peter's resolutions to break the news to his parents disappear when he sees his father.

Francey has to break through a great deal of academic red tape before she is finally accepted on the campus.

New York Herald Tribune, June 6, 1938

"The part of the pedagogue is made to order for Mr. Stewart. His diffident portrayal of a repressed fellow, who cuts loose in a series of revolts against conventions, lends humorous substance to sequences which are badly in want of it. Unless I am mistaken, he is one of the most knowing and engaging young actors appearing on the screeen at present. In this show, his role is definitely secondary, but he has the talent to realize every potentiality of the characterization and the good sense to keep it clearly in focus with the antic doings."

New Republic, June 22, 1938

"I've liked James Stewart's homely face since the first time I saw it: it wears well and gets better, and probably because he has in himself the true qualities of goodness he must describe."

Shopworn Angel

Shopworn Angel

DISTRIBUTOR: Loew's, Inc.
RUNNING TIME: 85 minutes
CAST: Margaret Sullavan, James Stewart, Walter Pidgeon, Hattie McDaniel, Nat Pendleton, Alan Curtis, Sam Levene, Eleanor Lynn, Carles D. Brown
PRODUCER: Joseph L. Mankiewicz
DIRECTOR: H. C. Potter
AUTHOR: Dana Burnet
SCREEN PLAY: Waldo Salt
CAMERAMAN: Joseph Ruttenberg
EDITOR: W. Don Hayes
REVIEWED: 6-29-38
RELEASED: 7-15-38

SYNOPSIS:

En route from the plains of Texas to a battlefield in France, Private Bill Pettigrew (Stewart) is stationed at Camp Merritt near New York City. One evening he collides with a limousine containing

With Walter Pidgeon, Margaret Sullavan in *The Shopworn Angel*

With Margaret Sullavan in *The Shopworn Angel*

glamorous Daisy Heath (Margaret Sullavan) whom he has always idolized.

Unaware of the nature of her attachment to her manager, Sam Bailey (Walter Pidgeon), Bill falls in love. Daisy marries Bill on the eve of his sailing to keep his ideal of her bright and shining. Bill is killed in action leaving Daisy and Sam to each other.

New York Herald Tribune, July 18, 1938

"In much the same manner James Stewart brings the Texan private to glowing life and keeps the characterization solid and appealing even when the script gives him little aid. Unless I am mistaken, *The Shopworn Angel* boasts two of the finest actors appearing on the screen today."

New Republic, July 11, 1938

"The human quality here is owing partly to the schooled restraint of writing and direction, but even more to the unaffected appeal and warmth of Margaret Sullavan, James Stewart and Walter Pidgeon."

". . . James Stewart is the deep slow yokel because he has created the illusion of a personal hurt and belief."

You Can't Take It With You

DISTRIBUTOR: Columbia
RUNNING TIME: 120 minutes
CAST: Jean Arthur, Lionel Barrymore, James Stewart, Edward Arnold, Mischa Auer, Ann Miller, Spring Byington, Samuel S. Hinds, Donald Meek, H. B. Warner, Halliwell Hobbes, Dub Taylor, Mary Forbes, Lillian Yarbo, Eddie Anderson, Clarence Wilson, Joseph Swickard, Ann Doran, Christian Rub, Bodil Rosing, Charles Lane, Harry Davenport
PRODUCER: Frank Capra
DIRECTOR: Frank Capra
AUTHORS: George S. Kaufman, Moss Hart
SCREEN PLAY: Robert Riskin
ART DIRECTOR: Stephen Goosson
MUSICAL SCORE: Dimitri Tiomkin
MUSICAL DIRECTOR: Morris Stoloff
CAMERAMAN: Joseph Walker
EDITOR: Gene Havlick
REVIEWED: 8-26-38
RELEASED: 9-29-38

With Jean Arthur on lobby poster of *You Can't Take It With You*

With Jean Arthur in *You Can't Take It With You*

64   The Films of James Stewart

With Ann Doran, Lionel Barrymore, Dub Taylor in *You Can't Take It With You*

SYNOPSIS:

Grandpa Vanderhof (Lionel Barrymore) is a rich, retired businessman who decided 30 years before that you can't take it with you. Since then he has been collecting stamps and friends. He is the grand patriarch of a crazy household including his daughter, Penny (Spring Byington) who started writing plays when a typewriter was left at the house by mistake, her husband, Paul (Samuel S. Hinds), who manufactures Roman Candles and rockets in the basement, and Penny's daughter Essie (Ann Miller) who does barefoot ballet under the direction of Kolenkhov (Mischa Auer), her Russian teacher.

Penny's daughter Alice (Jean Arthur) falls in love with Tony Kirby (Stewart) who is the son of a rich businessman, Anthony P. Kirby (Edward Arnold). Alice asks Tony's parents to dinner, but the Vanderhof residence and the sight of the household's shenanigans proves too much for the snobbish Kirbys. The Kirbys dash for home but are met at the door by two government men investigating the fireworks in the basement and they are all taken off to jail.

A sympathetic court frees everyone with a lecture, but an embarrassed Alice leaves home and Grandpa offers to sell his home to

With Edward Arnold in *You Can't Take It With You*

Kirby who wanted it all along as part of a big real estate deal. He offers his son Tony the presidency of a large firm, but he refuses wanting no part of the trickeries and ruthlessness of big business.

Mr. Kirby realizes that maybe Vanderhof has the right slant on life after all and changes from a stuffed shirt to a human being.

He gives the house back to Vanderhof. Alice comes back to Tony and everyone ends up happy.

New York Herald Tribune, September 2, 1938
"Wisdom and artistry have gone into the screen production of *You Can't Take It With You* to make an eminently satisfying entertainment. . . . James Stewart is fine as Tony Kirby . . . ."

Made For Each Other
DISTRIBUTOR: United Artists
RUNNING TIME: 85 minutes
CAST: Carole Lombard, James Stewart, Charles Coburn, Lucile Watson, Eddie Quillan, Alma Kruger, Ruth Weston, Donald Briggs,

With Carole Lombard in *Made For Each Other*

Harry Davenport, Esther Dale, Renee Orsell, Louise Beavers, Ward Bond, Olin Howland, Fern Emmett, Jackie Taylor, Mickey Rentschler, Ivan Simpson
PRODUCER: David O. Selznick
DIRECTOR: John Cromwell
SCREEN PLAY: Jo Swerling
ART DIRECTOR: Lyle Wheeler
MUSICAL DIRECTOR: Lou Forbes
CAMERAMAN: Leon Shamroy
SPECIAL EFFECTS: Jack Cosgrove
EDITORS: Hal C. Kern, James E. Newcom
REVIEWED: 2-6-39
RELEASED: 2-10-39

SYNOPSIS:

A young New York attorney, John Mason (Stewart) meets a girl, Jane (Carole Lombard), in Boston. They marry and he brings her home to his mother (Lucile Watson) who had plans for him to marry his employer's daughter.

The three share an apartment and the mother-in-law in residence is critical of Jane. John doesn't get the promotion he believes is due. His wife coaches him to lay down the law to his boss, Judge Doolittle (Charles Coburn). The boss anticipates the raise with a cut.

They have a baby, and not quite enough money to stay out of debt. So they decide to separate. The baby becomes ill with pneumonia. The baby needs serum and a nervy aviator, Conway (Eddie Quillan) flies the serum through a blizzard from Salt Lake City to New York.

The baby's recovery brings the family together and the hardhearted employer finally acknowledges John's ability.

Newsweek, February 13, 1939

"Perfectly cast in the leading roles, Carole Lombard and James Stewart are backed by a competent cast."

"While *Made for Each Other* is often as broad as it is subtle and compromises with showmanship in its melodramatic climax, it is never clumsy in its effective assault on the emotions."

Time, February 27, 1939

"*Made for Each Other* . . . acted, principally, by James Stewart

With Edwin Maxwell, Donald Briggs, Charles Coburn in *Made For Each Other*

With Carole Lombard in *Made For Each Other*

and Carole Lombard. Which of these deserves most credit for the indisputable fact that this mundane, domestic chronicle has more dramatic impact than all the hurricanes, sandstorms and earthquakes manufactured in Hollywood last season is a mystery which does not demand solution."

Ice Follies Of 1939

DISTRIBUTOR: Lowe's, Inc.
RUNNING TIME: 83 minutes
CAST: Joan Crawford, James Stewart, Lew Ayres, Lewis Stone, Bess Ehrhardt, Lionel Stander, Charles D. Brown, Roy Shipstad, Eddie Shipstad, Oscar Johnson
PRODUCER: Harry Rapf
DIRECTOR: Reinhold Schunzel
AUTHOR: Leonard Praskins
SCREEN PLAY: Leonard Praskins, Florence Ryerson, Edgar Allan Woolf
MUSICAL SCORE: Roger Edens
SCENIC EFFECTS: Merril Pye

It's a Wonderful World

SYNOPSIS:

Guy Johnson (Stewart) is a rather shady, but novice detective. He is assigned to watch over a millionaire playboy, Willie Heyward (Ernest Truex). Willie has too much to drink one night and finds himself with a murder rap. Guy is also named as an accessory and is on his way to prison by train. He escapes and is determined to find out the real killer and save his client.

Guy needs a car and takes one belonging to a lady poet, Edwina Corday (Claudette Colbert), and in the process kidnaps her. Guy runs through a series of disguises as a chauffeur, actor and Boy Scout leader in looking for evidence. Although Edwina is along unwillingly at first, she falls in love with him and continually gets Guy out of one mess after another. Guy finally gets all of his evidence together and discovers the real murderer, thus freeing his client.

New Republic, May 31, 1939

"*It's A Wonderful World* is, despite the title, one of the few genuinely comic pieces in a dog's age."

"James Stewart, Claudette Colbert, Nat Pendleton, Guy Kibbee, Edgar Kennedy. They're all good people in the right place, and they have it here."

With Guy Kibbee in *It's A Wonderful World*

With Rex Evans in *It's A Wonderful World*

With Edgar Dearing, Cecil Cunningham in *It's A Wonderful World*

Variety, May 17, 1939

"Whether or not Stewart's following, which has been built up to substantial proportions during the past year will accept him as an unchivalrous and woman-hating character, who eventually socks Miss Colbert on the jaw in a rather strained and unsurprising episode is a question."

Mr. Smith Goes To Washington

DISTRIBUTOR: Columbia
RUNNING TIME: 125 minutes
CAST: Jean Arthur, James Stewart, Claude Rains, Edward Arnold, Guy Kibbee, Thomas Mitchell, Eugene Pallette, Beulah Bondi, H. B. Warner, Harry Carey, Astrid Allwyn, Ruth Donnelly, Grant Mitchell, Porter Hall, Baby Dumpling, H. V. Kaltenborn, Pierre Watkin, Charles Lane, William Demarest, Dick Elliott, Billy Watson, Delmer Watson, John Russell, Harry Watson, Gary Watson.
PRODUCER: Frank Capra
DIRECTOR: Frank Capra
AUTHOR: Lewis R. Foster
SCREEN PLAY: Sidney Buchman
ART DIRECTOR: Lionel Banks
MUSICAL DIRECTOR: H. W. Stoloff
SCORE: Dimitri Tiomkin
CAMERAMAN: Joseph Walker
MONTAGE EFFECTS: Slavko Vorkapich
EDITORS: Gene Havlick, Al Clark
REVIEWED: 10-6-39
RELEASED: 10-16-39

SYNOPSIS:

Jefferson Smith (Stewart) is the idolized head of a chain of boys' clubs, the Boy Rangers. Governor Hopper (Guy Kibbee) and Political Boss Jim Taylor (Edward Arnold) think Jeff is the ideal Senator to cover up their graft. He is appointed to the Senate with the expectations that he will vote as the machine dictates. To be sure of this he takes orders from senior Senator Joseph Paine (Claude Rains).

Jeff's idealism and patriotism make him a laughing stock before the cynical press and Congress. He is eventually framed on misconduct charges and his spirit broken he is determined to go back to his boys' clubs. Jeff's hard-boiled secretary, Saunders (Jean Arthur), tells him why he was really sent to Washington. When the Senate meets to vote on his expulsion, Mr. Smith takes the floor in his own defense and stages a one-man filibuster for 23 hours, hoping to gain

74 The Films of James Stewart

In *Mr. Smith Goes to Washington*

With Jean Arthur, Thomas Mitchell in *Mr. Smith Goes to Washington*

With Jean Arthur in *Mr. Smith Goes to Washington*

With Claude Rains in *Mr. Smith Goes to Washington*

time to expose the corruption to the voters of his state.

Unnoticed at first he fights on and the galleries and the other Senators take notice for the first time. Senator Paine tries to shoot himself, then confesses to his guilt and Mr. Smith is exonerated behind a cheering gallery.

Theatre Arts, March, 1940

" . . . *Mr. Smith Goes to Washington* . . . reveals a degree of maturity in spirit, form and content which is seen but rarely in the product ground out of Hollywood's mill."

"But it is Capra's Mr. Smith, in the person of James Stewart, who endows the film with its richly appealing quality and gives it its emotional punch."

Time, October 23, 1939

"The acting of the brilliant cast is sometimes superb."

Newsweek, October 23, 1939

"With the exception of a few sorties into the extra-callow, James Stewart gives the most persuasive characterization of his career as a one-man crusade against political corruption."

Nation, October 28, 1939

" . . . far the best Hollywood picture of the year."

"James Stewart as Jefferson Smith takes first place among Hollywood actors."

" . . . Now he is mature and gives a difficult part, with many nuances, moments of tragi-comic impact. And he is able to do more than play isolated scenes effectively. He shows the growth of a character through experience. . . . In the end he is so forceful that his victory is thoroughly credible. One can only hope that after this success Mr. Stewart in Hollywood will remain as uncorrupted as Mr. Smith in Washington."

Destry Rides Again

DISTRIBUTOR: Universal
RUNNING TIME: 94 minutes
CAST: James Stewart, Charles Winninger, Brian Donlevy, Marlene Dietrich, Una Merkel, Irene Hervey, Jack Carson, Warren Hymer, Allen Jenkins, Samuel S. Hinds, Joe King, Mischa Auer, Billy Gilbert, Tom Fadden, Lillian Yarbo, Dickie Jones, Ann Todd
PRODUCER: Joseph Pasternak
DIRECTOR: George Marshall
AUTHOR: Max Brand

In *Destry Rides Again*

With Duke York (background), Marlene Dietrich in *Destry Rides Again*

SCREEN PLAY: Felix Jackson, Gertrude Purcell, Henry Myers
CAMERAMAN: Hal Mohr
EDITOR: Milton Carruth
REVIEWED: 11-30-39
RELEASED: 12-29-39

SYNOPSIS:

The picture takes place in the wide open cowtown of Bottle Neck in the wild West of the 1870s. The social and political center is the Last Chance saloon owned by Bottle Neck's hardest hombre, Kent (Brian Donlevy). He has a large following of cutthroats on his side as well as Frenchy (Marlene Dietrich), the painted songbird and gyp artist of Bottle Neck's toughest dive.

Frenchy and Kent combine to cheat in a card game and the sheriff is killed investigating the incident. The tophatted, tobacco-chewing crooked mayor, Hiram J. Slade (Samuel S. Hinds), appoints a new sheriff, Wash Dimsdale (Charles Winninger) the town drunk, just for laughs. Wash fools the town by taking his job seriously and states

With Marlene Dietrich in *Destry Rides Again*

With Mischa Auer, Samuel S. Hinds, Brian Donlevy, Warren Hymer, Duke York in *Destry Rides Again*

his new deputy will be Tom Destry (Stewart). Tom's father was a famous marshall and Wash was his deputy and he promptly sends for Tom who he feels will follow in his father's footsteps.

Wash is disappointed when Destry arrives minus guns and appears to make a fool of himself in front of Kent and his gang. Frenchy joins in the ridicule of Destry. Destry feels he can clean up Bottle Neck by using his head instead of his trigger finger. Wash is later killed and dies in the arms of Destry. Destry puts on his father's famous guns and goes to the Last Chance saloon joined by the townswomen armed with every conceivable type of weapon. They overpower the ruffians, but Kent escapes in the fracas, appears on the balcony and draws a bead on Destry. Frenchy slips in the saloon and realizes Destry's life is in danger. As Kent fires Frenchy desperately darts in front of Destry and is killed. Destry promptly shoots Kent and law is restored in Bottle Neck.

Newsweek, December 11, 1939
"Stewart brings humor and sound characterization to a boots-and-saddle variation of a typical Stewart role—the apparently easy-going softy who turns hard when it will do the most good."

Time, December 18, 1939
"James Stewart, who had just turned in the top performance of his cinematurity as Jefferson Smith in *Mr. Smith Goes to Washington,* turns in as good a performance or better as Thomas Jefferson Destry."

Variety, December 6, 1939
"Stewart's contribution has all the earmarks of a continuation of his *Mr. Smith Goes to Washington* characterization, but it's bound to register strongly with both the kids and femme customers."

The Shop Around the Corner
DISTRIBUTOR: Lowe's Inc.
RUNNING TIME: 97 minutes
CAST: Margaret Sullavan, James Stewart, Frank Morgan, Joseph Schildkraut, Sara Haden, Felix Bressart, William Tracy, Inez Courtney, Sarah Edwards, Edwin Maxwell, Charles Halton, Charles Smith
PRODUCER: Ernst Lubitsch
DIRECTOR: Ernst Lubitsch
AUTHOR: Nikolaus Lazzlo
SCREEN PLAY: Samson Raphaelson
ART DIRECTOR: Cedric Gibbons

With Margaret Sullavan in *The Shop Around The Corner*

With Margaret Sullavan in *The Shop Around The Corner*

With Margaret Sullavan in *The Shop Around The Corner*

With Margaret Sullavan in *The Shop Around The Corner*

MUSICAL SCORE: Werner R. Heymann
CAMERAMAN: William Daniels
EDITOR: Gene Ruggiero
REVIEWED: 1-8-40
RELEASED: 1-12-40

SYNOPSIS:

Alfred Kralik (Stewart) is a clerk in a leather goods and novelty shop owned by Hugo Matuschek (Frank Morgan) in Budapest. Kralik is in love and has been corresponding with an anonymous lonely heart who also happens to be working in the Shop, Klara Novak (Margaret Sullavan). Neither of them has the slightest idea that the other is the Dear Friend of the letters. They do not get along as co-workers and quarrel incessantly.

Hugo suspects Kralik of having an affair with his wife and when Kralik asks for time off to keep an appointment with the girl he has been corresponding with he is fired.

Hugo discovers it is another clerk, Ferencz Vadas (Joseph Schildkraut) who has been having the affair with his wife. He hires Kralik back with an increase in pay. Kralik discovers Klara is the girl of his letters and they realize that back of their unreasoning antagonism towards each other lies love.

New York Times, January 26, 1940

"James Stewart, Margaret Sullavan, Frank Morgan and Joseph Schildkraut make *The Shop Around the Corner* a pleasant place to browse in."

Time, February 5, 1940

"James Stewart walks through the amiable business of being James Stewart."

New Republic, February 19, 1940

"And since I think James Stewart is a young American with as broad and unaffected a base in a country's experience and joy as Huck Finn, I can let lame praise of him go by the board."

The Mortal Storm

DISTRIBUTOR: Loew's, Inc.
RUNNING TIME: 100 minutes
CAST: Margaret Sullavan, James Stewart, Robert Young, Frank Morgan, Robert Stack, Bonita Granville, Irene Rich, William T. Orr, Marie Ouspenskaya, Gene Reynolds, Russell Hicks, William Edmunds, Esther Dale, Dan Dailey, Jr., Granville Bates, Thomas

With Robert Young in *The Mortal Storm*

86   The Films of James Stewart

Ross, Ward Bond, Sue Moore, Harry Depp, Julius Tannen, Gus Glassmire
DIRECTOR: Frank Borzage
AUTHOR: Phyllis Bottome
SCREEN PLAY: Claudine West, Anderson Ellis, George Froeschel
MUSIC SCORE: Edward Kane
ART DIRECTOR: Cedric Gibbons
CAMERAMAN: William Daniels
EDITOR: Elmo Vernon
REVIEWED: 6-11-40
RELEASED: 6-14-40

SYNOPSIS:

This is the story of simple, kindly people suddenly faced with and trampled upon by the local hoodlums rising with the Nazi Party.

Professor Roth (Frank Morgan) lives in comfort and honor amid his family and students until Hitler comes to power. The beloved Jewish professor is then sent to a concentration camp and is later killed. His daughter, Freya (Margaret Sullavan) is engaged to Fritz Marberg (Robert Young). She breaks the engagement when Fritz

With Robert Young in *The Mortal Storm*

supports the Nazi regime. Farmer Martin Breitner (Stewart) loves Freya and he becomes an outcast when he opposes the brutality and regimentation of Naziism. He escapes to Austria but returns for Freya.

Fritz's sister Elsa (Bonita Granville) is forced to tell their plans and the storm troopers led by Fritz follow them into the mountains. As the two are about to cross the border to safety Freya is shot and killed and Martin carries her across the border in his arms.

New York Times, June 21, 1940

"It is magnificently directed and acted. James Stewart and Margaret Sullavan bring to vibrant and anguished life the two young people who resist the sweeping system."

New Republic, July 8, 1940

"Margaret Sullavan, James Stewart, Frank Morgan and Ouspenskaya are fine in their part of it."

Variety, June 12, 1940

"Performances are excellent, James Stewart is the courageous individualist who refuses to join the Nazi Party."

No Time For Comedy

DISTRIBUTOR: Warners
RUNNING TIME: 93 minutes
CAST: James Stewart, Rosalind Russell, Genevieve Tobin, Charles Ruggles, Allyn Joslyn, Clarence Kolb, Louise Beavers, J. M. Kerrigan Lawrence Grossmith, Robert Greig, Frank Faylen
PRODUCER: Jack L. Warner, Hal B. Wallis
ASSOCIATE PRODUCER: Robert Lord
DIRECTOR: William Keighley
AUTHOR: S. N. Behrman
SCREEN PLAY: Julius J. and Philip G. Epstein
CAMERAMAN: Ernie Haller
EDITOR: Owen Marks
REVIEWED: 9-9-40
RELEASED: 9-14-40

SYNOPSIS:

Gaylord Esterbrook (Stewart) is a newspaper writer from Minnesota. He writes a comedy about New York although he has never been there. Linda Paige (Rosalind Russell) is chosen as the leading lady. Gaylord is needed to make revisions and takes his first trip to the big city. Linda and Gaylord find a lot in common and they marry.

With Rosalind Russell in *No Time For Comedy*

In *No Time For Comedy*

With Ed Dearing, Allyn Joslyn in *No Time For Comedy*

With Allyn Joslyn, Herbert Heywood, Clarence Kolb in *No Time For Comedy*

90   The Films of James Stewart

Gaylord finds he has a real flair for comedy and writes four smashes in four years. Everything is going along fine until a rival, Amanda Swift (Genevieve Tobin) enters the scene.

She finds Gaylord attractive as she has found so many other men and convinces him that he has been wasting his time on comedy and that he should write a drama with a message. He believes her and tries his hand at a tragedy; and it ends up as this in more ways than one. He also thinks he is in love with Amanda. In order to get even, Linda starts seeing Amanda's husband, Philo Swift (Charles Ruggles).

The flop of his play brings Gaylord to his senses and he reconciles with his wife.

New York Times, September 7, 1940

"As usual, Mr. Stewart is the best thing in the show—a completely ingratiating character who ranges from the charming clumsiness of a country playwright to the temperamental distraction of an established writer with complete and natural assurance."

Variety, September 11, 1940

"Stewart, cast in a role which was obviously tailored to his measure, is topnotch in the characterization of the boyish playwright from the sticks who arrives in Manhattan with a map after detouring by way of the Grand Canyon because there was an excursion train running there."

The Philadephia Story

DISTRIBUTOR: Loew's, Inc.
RUNNING TIME: 112 minutes
CAST: Cary Grant, Katharine Hepburn, James Stewart, Ruth Hussey, John Howard, Roland Young, John Halliday, Mary Nash, Virginia Weidler, Henry Daniell, Lionel Pape, Rex Evans
PRODUCER: Joseph L. Mankiewicz
DIRECTOR: George Cukor
AUTHOR: Philip Barry
SCREEN PLAY: Donald Odgen Stewart
MUSICAL SCORE: Franz Waxman
ART DIRECTOR: Cedric Gibbons
CAMERAMAN: Joseph Ruttenberg
EDITOR: Frank Sullivan
REVIEWED: 11–26–40
RELEASED: 11–26–40

With Katharine Hepburn, Ruth Hussey in *The Philadelphia Story*

With Katharine Hepburn in *The Philadelphia Story*

SYNOPSIS:

The story concerns itself with the Lord family, socialites who live in a wealthy section of Philadelphia.

Tracy Lord (Katharine Hepburn) is scheduled to marry a self-made coal company executive, George Kittredge (John Howard). Tracy's first husband, C. K. Dexter Haven (Cary Grant), returns to save the social register reputation of his former in-laws from the threats of a newspaper publisher to expose "Papa" Lord's (John Halliday) illicit love unless his paper's representatives are admitted to the wedding. Tracy divorced Haven two years before due to his excessive drinking. Haven brings along a reporter from a "scoop" magazine, Macauley Connor (Stewart) and his camera assistant Liz Imbrie (Ruth Hussey).

The Lord family puts on a grand show of well-bred behavior to impress the company, especially Tracy and little sister Dinah (Virginia Weidler) and Uncle Willie (Roland Young) who fills in for the absent father. In the course of events snobbish Tracy begins to realize her first marriage failed due to her own deficiencies and with the help of a little too much to drink and a nude but innocent early morning swim with Connor her fiance George walks out. The marriage goes on as planned, but with Tracy and Haven as the bride and groom.

With Cary Grant in *The Philadelphia Story*

The Philadelphia Story 93

With John Halliday, Cary Grant, Katharine Hepburn in *The Philadelphia Story*

New York Herald Tribune, December 27, 1940
"Stewart, in the part of the snooping journalist who hates his job and wants to write real stuff, contributes most of the comedy to the show. His reaction to a snobbish society built on wealth is a delight to watch. In addition, he contributes some of the most irresistible romantic moments to the proceedings."

Newsweek, December 16, 1940
"James Stewart and Cary Grant are excellent in the co-starring assignments."

Time, January 20, 1941
"It further offered that amiably stringy young man, James Stewart . . . ."

New Republic, December 23, 1940
"Stewart keeps to his level of near-perfection as the impulsive, wrong-moving ordinary guy, and certainly adds another star to his honorchart for the whole sequence of moonlight and four roses."

Come Live With Me

DISTRIBUTOR: Loew's, Inc.
RUNNING TIME: 86 minutes
CAST: James Stewart, Hedy Lamarr, Ian Hunter, Verree Teasdale, Donald Meek, Barton MacLane, Edward Ashley, Ann Codee, King Baggot, Adeline DeWalt Reynolds, Frank Orth, Frank Faylen, Horace MacMahon, Greta Meyer
PRODUCER: Clarence Brown
DIRECTOR: Clarence Brown
AUTHOR: Virginia Van Upp
SCREEN PLAY: Patterson McNutt
CAMERAMAN: George Folsey
EDITOR: Frank E. Hull
REVIEWED: 1-30-41
RELEASED: 1-31-41

SYNOPSIS:

Johnny Jones (Hedy Lamarr) is a wealthy Austrian refugee about to be sent back to Hitler's Austria due to the immigration laws. She is in love with publisher Barton Kendrick (Ian Hunter) who al-

With Adeline DeWalt Reynolds in *Come Live With Me*

With Hedy Lamarr in *Come Live With Me*

With Donald Meek in *Come Live With Me*

In *Come Live With Me*

ready has a wife, Diana (Verree Teasdale). Barton wants to marry Johnny but needs time for a divorce.

Johnny is in need of an American husband and meets Bill Smith (Stewart) an aspiring young author sitting on a park bench with his last dime. Johnny has no desire to leave America and induces Bill to marry her. They keep separate residences and she pays Bill's rent and expenses, keeping her own address a secret.

Bill writes a story on the situation and it comes to Kendrick's attention. Bill locates Johnny and takes her to the country to the farm of his grandmother (Adeline de Walt Reynolds). With these surroundings Johnny falls in love with Bill despite Kendrick's valient effort to win her back.

New York Herald Tribune, February 28, 1941

"The film's final sequences are the most enjoyable, when Mr. Stewart takes his bargain-counter wife to the country to woo her under the spell of the out-of-doors and an indulgent grandmother."

"Mr. Stewart plays throughout with the easy assurance that has won for him so much respect."

Pot O' Gold

Pot O' Gold

DISTRIBUTOR: United Artists
RUNNING TIME: 86 minutes
CAST: James Stewart, Paulette Goddard, Horace Heidt, Charles Winninger, Mary Gordon, Frank Melton, Jed Prouty, Dick Hogan, James Burke, Charlie Arnt, Donna Wood, Larry Cotton, Henry Roquemore, William Gould, Aldrich Bowker
PRODUCER: James Roosevelt
DIRECTOR: George Marshall
AUTHORS: Monte Brice, Andrew Bennison, Harry Tugend
SCREEN PLAY: Walter De Leon
CAMERAMAN: Hal Mohr
EDITOR: Lloyd Nosler
REVIEWED: 4-4-41
RELEASED: 4-11-41

SYNOPSIS:

Jimmy Haskel (Stewart) is a harmonica playing music-mad youth who discovers a band of struggling musicians, (Horace Heidt and his Orchestra) who practice on the roof of a boarding house. The board-

With Charles Winninger, Charles Arnt in *Pot O' Gold*

With Paulette Goddard, Horace Heidt in *Pot O' Gold*

In *Pot O' Gold*

With Charles Winninger, Irving Bacon in *Pot O' Gold*

ing house is run by Mom McCorkle (Mary Gordon) and her pretty daughter, Molly (Paulette Goddard).

Jimmy joins the band and sides with them when his wealthy uncle, Charley Haskel (Charles Winninger) is annoyed by their practicing to the point where he takes legal action. Jimmy finally talks his uncle into putting new life into the radio program advertising his health foods and works the band into the show.

Molly accuses Jimmy of deception when he hides his identity and of exploiting the band for his own benefit. Jimmy solves all his problems when he comes up with the idea of the "Pot O' Gold" which gives away $1000 of his uncle's money every week to the accompaniment of Heidt's band.

Newsweek, April 7, 1941

"James Stewart not only gives an ingratiating performance as the harmonica-playing nephew of the music-hating food manufacturer but sings on the screen for the first time—and not at all badly.

Ziegfeld Girl

DISTRIBUTOR: Loew's, Inc.

100   The Films of James Stewart

RUNNING TIME: 131 minutes
CAST: James Stewart, Judy Garland, Hedy Lamarr, Lana Turner, Tony Martin, Jackie Cooper, Ian Hunter, Charles Winninger, Edward Everett Horton, Philip Dorn, Paul Kelly, Eve Arden, Dan Dailey, Jr., Al Shean, Fay Holden, Felix Bressart, Rose Hobart
PRODUCER: Pandro S. Berman
DIRECTOR: Robert Z. Leonard
AUTHOR: William Anthony McGuire
SCREEN PLAY: Marguerite Roberts, Sonya Levien
CAMERAMAN: Ray June
EDITOR: Blanche Sewell
REVIEWED: 4-16-41
RELEASED: 4-25-41

SYNOPSIS.

The story concerns itself with the triumphs and defeats of three girls chosen for the Follies.

Sheila Regan (Lana Turner) is spotted while running an elevator. An agent, Noble Sage (Edward Everett Horton), arrives to tell her she has been picked for the Follies. She is too stunned to

With Lana Turner, Fay Holden in *Ziegfeld Girl*

With Lana Turner in *Ziegfeld Girl*

With Lana Turner, Jackie Cooper in *Ziegfeld Girl*

With Elliott Sullivan, James Flavin in *Ziegfeld Girl*

speak and her boy friend Gilbert Young (Stewart) has to supply the answers. Success turns her head and she tries to decide between her boy friend, Gil and an aging socialite, Geoffrey Collis (Ian Hunter). Too much of a good thing proves too much for Sheila as she dies of a heart attack on opening night of a new edition of *Ziegfeld Follies* while Gil goes on to greater heights.

Sandra Kolter (Hedy Lamarr) joins the Follies and her husband, violinist Franz Kolter (Philip Dorn), leaves her protesting her action. She finally discovers he is more exciting than the Follies and wins him back.

Susan Gallagher (Judy Garland) makes it big as a singer and creates an opportunity for her father, Pop Gallagher (Charles Winninger) and his partner Al (Al Shean) to be a success in the show.

New York Times, April 24, 1941
 "Mr. Stewart is able as usual."

Newsweek, April 28, 1941
 ". . . and Gil Young, her truck-driver boy friend, a thankless role portrayed by James Stewart."

It's a Wonderful Life

It's a Wonderful Life

DISTRIBUTOR: RKO-Liberty
RUNNING TIME: 129 minutes
CAST: James Stewart, Donna Reed, Lionel Barrymore, Henry Travers, Beulah Bondi, Ward Bond, Frank Faylen, Gloria Grahame, H. B. Warner, Samuel S. Hinds, Frank Albertson, Virginia Patton, Todd Karns
PRODUCER: Frank Capra
DIRECTOR: Frank Capra
SCREEN PLAY: Frances Goodrich, Albert Hackett, Frank Capra
ART DIRECTOR: Jack Okey
MUSIC: Dimitri Tiomkin
CAMERAMEN: Joseph Walker, Joseph Biroc
EDITOR: William Hornbeck
REVIEWED: 12-19-46
RELEASED: 1-7-47

SYNOPSIS:

George Bailey (Stewart) of Bedford Falls is a small town boy who leads a very dull life working in his father's small building and loan company. His father, Pa Bailey (Samuel S. Hinds), dies leaving

With Al Hill, Frank Faylen, Donna Reed in *It's A Wonderful Life*

With William Edmunds, Stanley Andrews in *It's A Wonderful Life*

With Thomas Mitchell in *It's A Wonderful Life*

It's a Wonderful Life

With Mary Treen, Charles B. Williams, Charles Halton in *It's A Wonderful Life*

George to run the company. He marries his childhood sweetheart, Mary Hatch (Donna Reed) and settles down shackled to his family and in a deep rut. Running the business with his heart rather than his head he befriends his fellow men and shoulders the whole town's troubles.

The local banker, Dr. Potter (Lionel Barrymore), is a skinflint who would like to drive George to ruin. Uncle Billy (Thomas Mitchell), George's assistant, lets the company's bankroll fall into Potter's hands the night the bank examiner comes to look over his books. George is facing ruin, gets drunk, has suicidal tendencies and states "I wish I'd never been born." At this point he gets his wish as a guardian angel, Clarence (Henry Travers), appears and shows George what a dismal place Bedford Falls would have been without him. When he returns home finally realizing his importance to the town he further finds his friends have rallied to the cause by raising the needed money.

New York Times, December 23, 1946

"As the hero, Mr. Stewart does a warmly appealing job, indicating that he has grown in spiritual stature as well as in talent during the years he was in the war."

Nation, February 15, 1947

"In particular, the hero is extravagantly well played by James Stewart."

New Republic, January 6, 1947

"The postwar Jimmy Stewart looks a shade more mellow and works much harder at his acting, but he's still stuck in *It's a Wonderful Life* with his traditional character grown flat with usage--unassuming, a bit shy, sincere as a Boy Scout, a passionate spokesman for the little people."

Newsweek, December 30, 1946

"There are any number of knowing performances, but the topper is Stewart's adult, appealing, postwar impersonation of the frustrated stay-at-home who learns that wealth is measured in terms of people he can call friends."

Time, December 23, 1946

"Actor James Stewart has also boosted his rank as an actor. Having put aside his aggressively boyish, aw-shucks screen mannerisms, Stewart's first postwar performance is certain to be eyed respectfully by the people who award annual statuettes for superior acting."

Magic Town

DISTRIBUTOR: RKO
RUNNING TIME: 103 minutes
CAST: James Stewart, Jane Wyman, Kent Smith, Ned Sparks, Regis Toomey, Wallace Ford, Ann Doran, Donald Meek, E. J. Ballentine, Ann Shoemaker, Mickey Kuhn, Howard Freeman, Henry Polman, Mary Currier, Mickey Roth, Frank Fenton, George Irving, Julia Dean, Frank Darien, Robert Dudley
PRODUCER: Robert Riskin
DIRECTOR: William A. Wellman
AUTHORS: Robert Riskin, Joseph Krumgold
SCREEN PLAY: Robert Riskin
MUSICAL SCORE: Roy Webb
MUSICAL DIRECTOR: C. Bakaleinikoff
CAMERAMAN: Joseph F. Biroc
EDITORS: Sherman Todd, Richard Wray
REVIEWED: 8–27–47
RELEASED: 10–12–47

With Ned Sparks in *Magic Town*

With George Irving, Kent Smith in *Magic Town*

SYNOPSIS:

Rip Smith (Stewart) is a failure as a public opinion expert until he discovers a mathematical miracle in a town called Grandview. The population thinks on every subject just as the experts say the public thinks. He and Ike Sloan (Ned Sparks) establish themselves in the town as insurance salesmen polling the community in the process.

He falls in love with the editor of the local newspaper, Mary Peterman (Jane Wyman). She learns his real occupation and exposes him. As a result the town booms, as the news media exploits it as a typical town. Values go up including real estate as the townspeople try to cash in on its sudden fame. They all hit bottom when the bubble bursts.

A remorseful Rip rallies the townsfolk and redeems the town's spirit and is forgiven by the girl editor.

New York Herald Tribune, October 8, 1947

"Stewart's portrayal of a poll-taker who plays a mean trick on some nice people and then becomes remorseful enough to save them from their folly is both energetic and likeable. Sometimes he distorts his performance by working his role for more eccentricity than

In *Magic Town*

With Tom Kennedy, William Haade, Frank Marlowe, Selmar Jackson, Ned Sparks, Richard Wessel in *Magic Town*

it actually contains, but he makes good fun out of such business as coaching the local school basketball team or storming into the small-town newspaper office to make a complaint."

Time, October 20, 1947

"*Magic Town* is another of those seriocomic fables in favor of the American way of life which, it appears cannot be made without James Stewart."

Call Northside 777

DISTRIBUTOR: 20th Century-Fox
RUNNING TIME: 111 minutes
CAST: James Stewart, Richard Conte, Lee J. Cobb, Helen Walker, Helen Garde, Kasia Orzazewski, Jeanne de Bergh, Howard Smith, Moroni Olsen, John McIntire, Paul Harvey, J. M. Kerrigan, Samuel S. Hinds, George Tyne, Richard Bishop, Otto Waldis, Michael Chapin, John Bleifer, Addison Richards, Richard Rober, Eddie Dunn, Percy Helton, Charles Lane, Jane Crawley, E. G. Marshall, Lou Eckels
PRODUCER: Otto Lang

With Richard Rober in *Call Northside 777*

With Henry Kulky in *Call Northside 777*

Call Northside 777

In *Call Northside 777*

DIRECTOR: Henry Hathaway
AUTHOR: James P. McGuire
SCREEN PLAY: Jerome Cady, Jay Dratler
ART DIRECTORS: Lyle Wheeler, Mark-Lee Kirk
PHOTOGRAPHY: Joe MacDonald
EDITOR: J. Watson Webb, Jr.
REVIEWED: 1-21-48
RELEASED: February, 1948

SYNOPSIS:
Frank Wiecek (Richard Conte) is charged with the murder of a policeman in 1932 and sentenced to 99 years in the state penitentiary. His mother, Tillie (Kasia Orzazewski), has scrubbed floors for almost 11 years to raise $5000 so she can run an ad offering $5000 for information leading to the real killers.

The city editor, Brian Kelly (Lee J. Cobb), assigns reporter McNeal (Stewart) to look into the ad. He interviews Tillie and has no doubts that her son is guilty. He prints her story only for the human interest and good "copy."

As McNeal pursues the mother further he eventually begins to

With Richard Conte in *Call Northside 777*

understand Tillie's faith in her son and becomes convinced that he is innocent. Through his newspaper he soon has much of the city with him with the exception of a hostile police force. McNeal has to steal evidence from the cops, wander through menacing slums in tracking down a witness who had perjured herself on the stand. His evidence finally clears Wiecek after he had served 13 years. The film was based on a true story.

New York Times, February 19, 1948
   "Furthermore, it is winningly acted by James Stewart as the reporter-sleuth. . . ."

New York Herald Tribune, February 19, 1948
   "The performances, from James Stewart's characterization of an inquisitive reporter to the merest bits, have honesty and persuasion."
   "Since Stewart plays the original James P. McGuire, whose articles inspired the film, with intensity and occasional flashes of humor, he keeps the treads of the script from becoming badly tangled."
   "Although Stewart obviously dominates the action, the large supporting cast lends credence and excitement to the proceedings."

Time, February 16, 1948
   "James Stewart manages to mug a little now and then, but by and large his performance is exceptionally modest, and as good as his best."

On Our Merry Way

On Our Merry Way

DISTRIBUTOR: United Artists—Bogeaus
RUNNING TIME: 107 minutes
CAST: Burgess Meredith, Paulette Goddard, Fred MacMurray, Hugh Herbert, James Stewart, Henry Fonda, Dorothy Lamour, Victor Moore, Eilene Janssen, William Demarest, Dorothy Ford, Charles D. Brown, Betty Caldwell, David Whorf, Frank Moran, Tom Fadden, Paul Hurst
PRODUCERS: Benedict Bogeaus, Burgess Meredith
DIRECTORS: King Vidor, Leslie Fenton
AUTHOR: Arch Oboler
SCREEN PLAY: Laurence Stalling
ART DIRECTORS: Ernst Fegte, Duncan Cramer
MUSICAL SUPERVISORS: David Chudnow, Skitch Henderson
PHOTOGRAPHY: Edward Cronjager, Joseph Biroc, Gordon Avil, John Seitz
EDITOR: James Smith
REVIEWED: 2-2-48 (reviewed as "A Miracle Can Happen")
RELEASED: June 1948

With Eduardo Cianelli, Henry Fonda, Carl Switzer in *On Our Merry Way*

SYNOPSIS:

Oliver Pease (Burgess Meredith) is a classified want-ad clerk on a Los Angeles newspaper who thinks he is a writer. He impersonates his paper's roving reporter for a day. Martha Pease (Paulette Goddard) gives him his questions for the day and the result is three stories.

Oliver first comes upon Slim (Stewart) and Lank (Henry Fonda) who are two musicians trying to earn a much-needed buck by fixing an amateur music contest at a California beach resort for the mayor's son.

The second story has Gloria Manners (Dorothy Lamour) and Ashton Carrington (Victor Moore) playing Hollywood "extras" down on their luck.

The third story has Al (Fred MacMurray) and Floyd (William Demarest) as a couple of drifters who are at the mercy of a little boy who delights in playing practical jokes on them. The boy's rich uncle, Elisha Hobbs (Hugh Herbert), insists on receiving money rather than paying for the return of the boy.

New York Times, February 4, 1948

"Mr. Stewart and Mr. Fonda whip a purely ridiculous script into an act of low-comedy mugging that is a good bit of slapstick fun."

With Henry Fonda in *On Our Merry Way*

Rope 115

New Republic, February 23, 1948

"The first of the one-acters, written by John O'Hara and starring James Stewart and Henry Fonda shows some life."

Newsweek, February 16, 1948

"Fonda and Stewart get the film off to a hilarious, frankly slapstick start."

Rope

DISTRIBUTOR: Warners-Trans Atlantic
RUNNING TIME: 80 minutes
CAST: James Stewart, John Dall, Farley Granger, Sir Cedric Hardwicke, Constance Collier, Douglas Dick, Edith Evanston, Dick Hogan, Joan Chandler
PRODUCER-DIRECTOR: Alfred Hitchcock
AUTHOR: Patrick Hamilton
SCREEN PLAY: Arthur Laurents
ART DIRECTOR: Perry Ferguson
MUSICAL DIRECTOR: Leo F. Forbstein
PHOTOGRAPHY: Joseph Valentine, William V. Skall

With John Dall in *Rope*

With Edith Evanson in *Rope*

With John Dall, Joan Chandler in *Rope*

EDITOR: William H. Zieger
REVIEWED: 8–26–48
RELEASED: 9–25–48

SYNOPSIS:

Rupert Cadell (Stewart) is the headmaster of a school and preaches a philosophy of superior human beings. Brandon (John Dall) and Philip (Farley Granger) attended the school. They murder a friend for the thrill of it, stuff his body in an old chest and set out to prove their superiority with a perfect crime—since there was no motive.

In their wealthy apartment they decide to serve a buffet supper on the chest in which the body is stuffed. They invite Mr. Kentley (Sir Cedric Hardwicke) the boy's father, Janet (Joan Chandler), his fiancee and as a final test their former school master, Cadell.

At the supper Philip begins to crack even though Brandon is caught up in his imagined superiority. Cadell becomes suspicious, returns to the apartment, pieces together the crime and how it was committed. He confronts the boys and waits for the police to arrive.

The Films of James Stewart

With John Dall in *Rope*

New York Morning Telegraph, August 27, 1948

"Mr. Stewart also makes as much as he can out of this particular assignment, but I'm afraid he was engaged for this task more for the lustre of his own name than for any adaptability he might have for the part."

New Republic, September 13, 1948

"Stewart's role, however suffers from a deadly implausibility."

Variety, September 1, 1948

"James Stewart, as the ex-professor who first senses the guilt of his former pupils and nibbles away at their composure with verbal barbs does a commanding job."

You Gotta Stay Happy

DISTRIBUTOR: Universal-International-Rampart
RUNNING TIME: 100 minutes
CAST: Joan Fontaine, James Stewart, Eddie Albert, Roland Young, Willard Parker, Percy Kilbride, Porter Hall, Marcy McGuire, Arthur Walsh, William Bakewell, Paul Cavanaugh, Halliwell Hobbes, Stanley Prager, Mary Forbes, Edith Evanson, Houseley

You Gotta Stay Happy

With Eddie Albert, Joan Fontaine in *You Gotta Stay Happy*

Stevenson, Emory Parnell, Don Kohler, Bert Conway, Hal K. Dawson, Vera Marshe, Jimmie Dodd, Robert Rockwell

PRODUCER: Karl Tunberg
DIRECTOR: H. C. Potter
AUTHOR: Robert Carson
SCREEN PLAY: Karl Tunberg
MUSIC: Daniele Amfitheatrof
ART DIRECTOR: Alexander Golitzen
PHOTOGRAPHY: Russell Metty, Paul Weatherwax
REVIEWED: 10-28-48
RELEASED: January 1949

SYNOPSIS:

Dee Dee Dillwood (Joan Fontaine), heiress, can't make up her mind about marriage. She finally marries Henry Benson (Willard Parker). On her honeymoon in New York she's not quite sure she married the right man. She's afraid to enter the bedroom of her husband and hides out in the bedroom of the adjoining hotel suite occupied by Marvin Payne (Stewart). Marvin is a dedicated flyer who is about to go bankrupt with his two-plane cargo outfit.

Dee Dee complicates things by taking sleeping pills. She can not

With Eddie Albert in *You Gotta Stay Happy*

With Joan Fontaine in *You Gotta Stay Happy*

With Joan Fontaine in *You Gotta Stay Happy*

be awakened enough to leave the hotel under her own power and Payne and his co-pilot, Bullets Baker (Eddie Albert) are forced to take her to California with them.

In order to make the trip pay they add an escaped embezzler, Mr. Carson (Porter Hall), a G. I. and his bride (Arthur Walsh and Marcy McGuire), a corpse, a shipment of whitefish, lobsters and a cigar-smoking chimpanzee. They make a forced landing and are aided by farmer Racknell (Percy Kilbride). Through the course of events Dee Dee worms her way into Payne's heart and the business.

New York Times, November 5, 1948

"James Stewart, to our mind, shows up much better in *You Gotta Stay Happy* than in any of his previous post-war efforts."

Time, November 22, 1948

"This is the kind of role that Jimmy Stewart could play blindfolded, hog-tied and in the bottom of a well. He gives it all the best Stewartisms."

Variety, November 3, 1948

"Miss Fontaine and Stewart play it ably for laughs."

The Stratton Story

DISTRIBUTOR: Metro-Goldwyn-Mayer
RUNNING TIME: 106 minutes
CAST: James Stewart, June Allyson, Frank Morgan, Agnes Moorehead, Bill Williams, Bruce Cowling, Cliff Clark, Mary Lawrence, Dean White, Robert Gist, Gene Bearden, Bill Dickey, Jimmy Dykes, Mervyn Shea
PRODUCER: Jack Cummings
DIRECTOR: Sam Wood
SCREEN PLAY: Douglas Morrow, Guy Trosper
AUTHOR: Douglas Morrow
PHOTOGRAPHY: Harold Rosson
EDITOR: Ben Lewis
MUSIC: Adolph Deutsch
REVIEWED: 4-12-49
RELEASED: 4-20-49

SYNOPSIS:

Monty Stratton (Stewart) is discovered in a sandlot baseball game by a has-been Barney Wile (Frank Morgan) and Barney develops him into a brilliant pitcher. He makes the big leagues with the

With June Allyson in *The Stratton Story*

With Agnes Moorehead, June Allyson in *The Stratton Story*

White Sox, but his bright future is suddenly and tragically darkened by a leg injury as a result of a hunting accident.

His wife Ethel (June Allyson) has to decide for or against amputation. His leg is amputated above the knee and he loses interest and will have nothing to do with his artificial limb. He stares into space, brooding over his lost career while Ethel and Monty's mother (Agnes Moorehead) wait for him to get over his misfortune.

He sees his young son trying to learn to walk and they take their first steps together. This is the turning point and he learns to use his artificial leg, regains his pitching form, and gets himself into a professional game to see where he stands. He wins and gains the needed confidence for the future.

New York Times, May 13, 1949

"*The Stratton Story* was the best thing that has yet happened to Mr. Stewart in his post-war film career. . . . Mr. Stewart gives such a winning performance that it is almost impossible to imagine anyone else playing the role."

New York Herald Tribune, May 13, 1949

"The redoubtable James Stewart has turned baseball player in

With Frank Morgan, Jimmy Dykes in *The Stratton Story*

With Frank Morgan in *The Stratton Story*

The Stratton Story. Thanks to his engaging and artful performance, a sentimental and inspirational screen biography has more than a little power."

Good Housekeeping, June 1949

"The Stratton is lanky Monty, one of baseball's living greats, played by gangly Jimmy Stewart just about to perfection."

New Republic, May 30, 1949

"James Stewart, as the young Stratton, plays the pitching phenomenon from the back country with a pleasant Will Rogers wit, and in the ball-park sequences looks astonishingly like a professional."

Newsweek, May 23, 1949

"Stewart gives a restrained and understanding performance in the title role."

Time, May 9, 1949

"Jimmy Stewart plays Monty and, under Stratton's coaching, does a good deal of plausible hurling without calling in a double. Except for a bit of sly mugging in the early scenes, Stewart turns in a solid, heart-warming performance."

Malaya

DISTRIBUTOR: M-G-M
RUNNING TIME: 98 minutes
CAST: Spencer Tracy, James Stewart, Valentina Cortesa, Sydney Greenstreet, John Hodiak, Lionel Barrymore, Gilbert Roland, Roland Winters, Richard Loo, Ian MacDonald, Tom Helmore
PRODUCER: Edwin H. Knopf
DIRECTOR: Richard Thorpe
SCREEN PLAY: Frank Fenton (based on story by Manchester Boddy)
REVIEWED: 12–5–49
RELEASED: 1–6–50

SYNOPSIS:

Rubber is needed in World War II for our armed forces. A plan and manpower is needed to smuggle it out from under the Japanese noses on Malaya. John Royer (Stewart) a newspaper reporter is chosen for his knowledge of the island. It is also necessary to have the services of a crackerjack smuggler who has some useful contacts. Carnahan (Spencer Tracy) who is serving a life term in Alcatraz is chosen.

A middleman is needed and an untrustworthy fellow is chosen known as The Dutchman (Sydney Greenstreet). He furnishes information on hidden stockpiles of rubber and their owners.

After completing his role in *Malaya*

With Sydney Greenstreet, Spencer Tracy in *Malaya*

With Spencer Tracy, Valentina Cortesa, Sydney Greenstreet in *Malaya*

Royer and Carnahan manage to get 150,000 tons of rubber out in two shipments with the aid of our own Navy, but run into trouble with the final trip when the Japanese commander, Colonel Genichi Tomura (Richard Loo), becomes suspicious. He ambushes the fleet carrying the rubber and Royer is killed. Carnahan is wounded but manages to get the cargo down river and into the United States ships.

New York Herald Tribune, January 23, 1950

"For all of Stewart's artful acting, Tracy dominates the film from beginning to end."

New York Times, January 23, 1950

"A rousing, old-fashioned thriller about bold men with wily minds and crushing fists with Spencer Tracy, James Stewart and Sydney Greenstreet acting in top form."

Winchester '73

DISTRIBUTOR: Universal
RUNNING TIME: 92 minutes
CAST: James Stewart, Shelley Winters, Dan Duryea, Stephen McNally, Millard Mitchell, Charles Drake, John McIntire, Will Geer, Jay C. Flippen, Rock Hudson, John Alexander, Steve

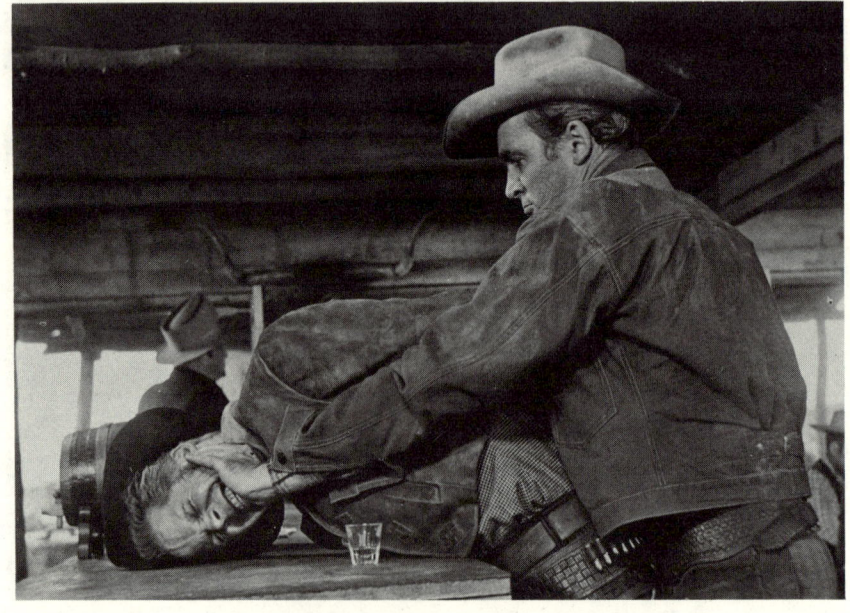

With Dan Duryea in *Winchester '73*

With Millard Mitchell in *Winchester '73*

With Millard Mitchell, Tony Curtis, Charles Drake, Jay C. Flippen in *Winchester '73*

The Films of James Stewart

In *Winchester '73*

Brodie, James Millican, Abner Biberman, Tony Curtis, James Best
PRODUCER: Aaron Rosenberg
DIRECTOR: Anthony Mann
SCREEN PLAY: Robert L. Richards, Borden Chase
STORY: Stuart N. Lake
REVIEWED: June 1950
RELEASED: 6-8-50

SYNOPSIS:

Lin McAdam (Stewart) and his sidekick High Spade (Millard Mitchell) ride into Dodge City in 1873. Vengeance is their motive as they are looking for the killer of McAdam's father. In a Dodge City marksmanship contest McAdam wins a Winchester '73 repeater that is in a class of its own. He defeats Dutch Henry Brown (Stephen McNally) who is really the killer of McAdam's father. Brown later steals the weapon and skips town.

Brown loses the weapon to Joe Lamont (John McIntire), an Indian trader, in a game of cards. Lamont later loses the gun as well as his scalp to an Indian Chief. A later Indian raid on a cavalry detachment causes the rifle to change hands again as the chief is killed. Cowardly Steve Miller (Charles Drake) temporarily gets the rifle but is soon killed by highwayman Waco Johnny Dean (Dan Duryea) who relinquishes it back to the original thief, Brown. Meanwhile McAdam and his pal are still pursuing the weapon and the killer. McAdam corners Brown on a mountain top and a blazing gun duel follows. McAdam kills Brown, avenging his father's death, and gets his prize rifle back.

New York Herald Tribune, June 8, 1950

"Stewart takes to horses and fast shooting as though he had been doing nothing else throughout his illustrious career."

New York Times, June 8, 1950

"As the cowboy hero, Mr. Stewart drawls and fumbles comically, recalling his previous appearance as a diffident cowpoke in *Destry Rides Again.*"

Broken Arrow

DISTRIBUTOR: 20th Century-Fox
RUNNING TIME: 93 minutes
CAST: James Stewart, Jeff Chandler, Debra Paget, Basil Ruysdael,

In *Broken Arrow*

Will Geer, Joyce MacKenzie, Arthur Hunnicutt, Raymond Bramley, Jay Silverheels, Argentina Brunetti, Jack Lee, Robert Adler, Harry Carter, Robert Griffin, Bill Wilkerson, Mickey Kuhn, Chris Willow Bird, J. W. Cody, John War Eagle, Charles Soldani, Iron Eyes Cody, Robert Foster Dover, John Marston, Edwin Rand, John Doucette

PRODUCER: Julian Blaustein
DIRECTOR: Delmer Daves
SCREEN PLAY: Michael Blankfort (based on the novel "Blood Brother" by Elliott Arnold)
REVIEWED: 6-14-50
RELEASED: August 1950

SYNOPSIS:

The story takes place in Arizona around 1870 when the Chiricahua Apaches were on the war path. Civil war veteran Tom Jeffords (Stewart), now a scout, is disgusted about the wars and mistreatment of the Indians so he decides to try to make peace. He learns Apache dialect and customs and rides alone in search of Cochise (Jeff Chandler), leader of the Apaches. No white man has seen Cochise in the last ten years and survived.

Jeffords locates Cochise and the chief realizes the futility of warring with the whites, but his own family had been killed during a previous peace. He does agree to let the U. S. Mails go through. Jeffords begins to understand and respect the Apaches and their fight for survival. He falls in love with an Indian girl, Sonseeahray (Debra Paget) and they are married Apache style.

The truce is tested for three months prior to a final peace, but renegade Apaches attack the stage coach and are driven away by Cochise's warriors. Renegade whites attack Cochise and Sonseeahray is killed, but not in vain as peace finally does come.

New York Herald Tribune, July 21, 1950
"Stewart plays a self-appointed go-between in the war between the whiteman and the Apaches in the days just before Geronimo's activities. He is not at his best in the Western form, but he manages to play the story straight. . . ."

New York Times, July 21, 1950
"Mr. Stewart is a human specimen of miserable account. He fumbles his words, waves his hands in lazy gestures and throws his whole enterprise on a casual plane. This is all the more disconcerting when he is supposed to fall beautifully in love with a China-doll Indian maiden, whom Debra Paget rhapsodically plays."

In *Broken Arrow*

With Debra Paget, Jeff Chandler, Argentina Brunetti in *Broken Arrow*

Newsweek, August 7, 1950

"Remarkably sensitive performances by both Stewart and Chandler put the finishing touch on what is undoubtedly one of the most emotionally satisfying Westerns since *Stagecoach* and *The Virginian.*"

Saturday Review, August 5, 1950

"Jeff Chandler . . . steals the picture away from Jimmy, who always seems on the verge of saying to the cameraman, 'Aw, gee, fellows, let's go back and play baseball.' In *Destry Rides Again* Jimmy wasn't embarrassed by Marlene Dietrich, and he slapped leather in that one very well. Jimmy is never quite at ease in the love affair with Sonseeahray, played by Debra Paget."

The Jackpot

DISTRIBUTOR: 20th Century-Fox
RUNNING TIME: 85 minutes
CAST: James Stewart, Barbara Hale, James Gleason, Fred Clark, Alan Mowbray, Patricia Medina, Natalie Wood, Tommy Rettig, Robert Gist, Lyle Talbot, Charles Tannen, Bigelow Sayre, Dick Cogan,

The Jackpot

Jewel Rose, Eddie Firestone, Estelle Etterre, Claude Stroud, Caryl Lincoln, Valerie Mark, Joan Miller, Walter Baldwin, Syd Saylor, John Qualen, Fritz Feld, Kathryn Sheldon, Robert Dudley, Billy Wayne, Minerva Urecal, Milton Parsons, Kim Spaulding, Dulce Daye, Andrew Tombes

PRODUCER: Sam Engel
DIRECTOR: Walter Lang
SCREEN PLAY: Phoebe and Henry Ephron
PHOTOGRAPHY: Joseph LaShelle
EDITOR: J. Watson Webb
REVIEWED: 9–28–50
RELEASED: 10–2–50

SYNOPSIS:

Bill Lawrence (Stewart) is a small-town department store executive with a wife, Amy (Barbara Hale), and two children, Phyllis (Natalie Wood) and Tommy (Tommy Rettig). He receives a phone call telling him he is going to be called as a contestant for the "Name the Mystery Husband" program. Bill phones a reporter friend, Harry Summers (James Gleason) for some type of clue to the answer.

With James Gleason in *The Jackpot*

With Barbara Hale in *The Jackpot*

With Alan Mowbray, Barbara Hale in *The Jackpot*

With Robert Gist, Barbara Hale in *The Jackpot*

All of Bill's family and friends gather at his home awaiting the call and are on hand to congratulate him on his good fortune when he provides the correct answer. Bill is a happy man but not for long.

His home is suddenly swamped with $24,000 worth of merchandise ranging from 7,500 cans of Campbell's soup, a Shetland pony, 12 wrist watches, a portable swimming pool, $4,000 worth of shrubbery and all kinds of electrical gadgets. His troubles are only beginning as he learns he has to pay income tax on the merchandise. He is in the doghouse with his wife as one of the prizes is a beautiful artist, Hilda (Patricia Medina), who comes to paint his portrait. A strange-looking interior decorator, Leslie (Alan Mowbray) disturbs the household further trying to redecorate the living room and Bill's boss, Mr. Woodruff (Fred Clark) threatens to fire him. He even gets involved with a bookie when trying to sell some loot and gets in trouble with the police before he gets back to his normal life and a happy ending.

New Republic, December 11, 1950

"Stewart is possessed of one of the most ingratiating slow takes in Hollywood."

Newsweek, November 13, 1950

"The story never goes far away from its single situation and in the end relies heavily on its players—in particular on Stewart's deftly comic impersonation of a young man with a cornucopia."

Time, November 27, 1950

". . . but what keeps *Jackpot* moving briskly to its happy ending is the ingratiating acting of Jimmy Stewart."

New York Herald Tribune, November 23, 1950

"It is to James Stewart's considerable credit that he turns himself into a strong viewing-glass for the burlesque."

". . . Stewart makes a perfect picture of a man who has won an elephant on a bet."

Harvey

DISTRIBUTOR: Universal
RUNNING TIME: 103 minutes
CAST: James Stewart, Josephine Hull, Peggy Dow, Charles Drake, Cecil Kellaway, Victoria Horne, Jesse White, William Lynn, Wallace Ford, Nana Bryant, Grace Mills, Clem Bevans, Ida Moore

With Cecil Kellaway in *Harvey*

Harvey

With Clem Bevans in *Harvey*

PRODUCER: John Beck
DIRECTOR: Henry Koster
SCREEN PLAY: Mary Chase, Oscar Brodney
AUTHOR: Mary Chase
PHOTOGRAPHY: William Daniels
EDITOR: Ralph Dawson
MUSIC: Frank Skinner
REVIEWED: 10–10–50
RELEASED: 10–13–50

SYNOPSIS:

Elwood P. Dowd (Stewart) is a gentle, but slightly inebriated philosopher who enjoys bringing happiness to others. One night while bringing home a sick friend from Charlie's place he meets a "Pooka," or giant rabbit in this case, leaning against a lamp post. Since that night the invisible creature that he calls Harvey has been his constant companion and principal joy.

Elwood's sister, Veta Louise Simmons (Josephine Hull), has been trying to marry off her daughter, Myrtle (Victoria Horne), and is disturbed about her brother and feels that his presence around

With Harry Hines in *Harvey*

Harvey 141

the house talking to his friend will scare away suitors and alarm her friends. Besides she's beginning to see Harvey now and then herself. Desperate, she tries to have her brother committed to Chumley's Rest Home, run by an eminent psychiatrist Dr. Chumley (Cecil Kellaway).

With Harvey's help Veta finds she is the one that is committed instead of Elwood. Elwood soon has Dr. Chumley believing in Harvey and he even wants to borrow him for awhile. Veta is released and she refuses to let Dr. Chumley give Elwood a serum that will make Harvey disappear, as she realizes she doesn't want him to be a normal human being.

Library Journal, November 15, 1950
"As the generous and pleasant Elwood, James Stewart gives one of his finest performances."

New Republic, January 15, 1951
"In the movie, Stewart is OK, and that is about the size of it."

Newsweek, December 25, 1950
"Although Stewart lacks the precision timing and the delicately

With Josephine Hull in *Harvey*

deranged humor that Frank Fay brought to the original Elwood, his amiable, gregarious eccentric is very satisfactory substitute."

Saturday Review, January 6, 1951

"James Stewart's Elwood does lack some of the magic of Frank Fay's wizened creation, perhaps because Mr. Stewart just doesn't look like the kind of man who ever spent much time in a barroom. Then too, as the years lurch on, Mr. Stewart has an increasing though understandable inclination just to be himself."

Time, January 1, 1951

"In his place (Fay), James Stewart, who has also played the role on the stage, gives an able actor's performance, but one that subtly dilutes the quality of the whole play."

"Dowd takes on the coloration of Stewart's movie personality: the gangling awkwardness, the fumbling, apologetic gestures, the verbal false starts."

New York Times, December 22, 1958

"As Elwood P. Dowd, Mr. Stewart is utterly beguiling and disarming of all annoyance. . . . Mr. Stewart makes Elwood a man to be admired."

No Highway in the Sky

DISTRIBUTOR: Twentieth Century-Fox
RUNNING TIME: 99 minutes
CAST: James Stewart, Marlene Dietrich, Glynis Johns, Jack Hawkins, Ronald Squire, Janette Scott, Niall McGinnis, Kenneth More, David Hutcheson, Ben Williams, Maurice Denham, Wilfrid Hyde White, Hector McGregor, Basil Appleby, Michael Kingsley, Peter Murray, Elizabeth Allan, Dora Bryan
PRODUCER: Louis D. Lighton
DIRECTOR: Henry Koster
SCREEN PLAY: R. C. Sherriff, Oscar Millard, Alec Coppel
AUTHOR: Nevil Shute
PHOTOGRAPHY: Georges Perinal
EDITOR: Manuel del Campo
REVIEWED: 6-28-51
RELEASED: 7-8-51

SYNOPSIS:

Mr. Honey (Stewart) is an eccentric, absent-minded scientist who is an engineer in the Royal Aircraft Establishment. He is convinced that the tail assembly of the Reindeer, a new type of aircraft, will snap from metal fatigue after 1,440 flying hours. His boss,

With Jack Hawkins, Janette Scott in *No Highway in the Sky*

With Marlene Dietrich in *No Highway in the Sky*

Dennis Scott (Jack Hawkins), sends him to Labrador to investigate a crash of one of the new planes. Officials will not ground the plane until they are sure Mr. Honey is not crazy.

He discovers the plane he is on is a Reindeer and almost to the critical amount of flying hours. The pilot refuses to turn back. He is humored by the stewardess, Marjorie Corder (Glynis Johns), and he warns Monica Teasdale (Marlene Dietrich), a movie-star, of their danger. The plane reaches Gander, Newfoundland, and is given a thorough check that confirms its airworthiness. Mr. Honey wrecks the aircraft on the ground. He is sent back to England and considered out of his mind. His sincerity convinces Marjorie and Monica he is sane and they follow to help clear him. He is completely vindicated when his calculations are proven to be correct.

Catholic World, October, 1951

"James Stewart may be a bit too ten-thumbed as the slow-talking hero but it is an appealing characterization which no one does better than he."

Saturday Review, October 6, 1951

"Mr. Stewart, Miss Dietrich, and Miss Johns are remarkably appealing personalities, and they are at their very best here."

With Glynis Johns in *No Highway in the Sky*

With Glynis Johns, Marlene Dietrich in *No Highway in the Sky*

New York Herald Tribune, September 22, 1951

"Playing Mr. Honey, Stewart walks in a bent-over position as though he were approaching a microscope to peer into it and in like manner leads his acting with all the fussy paraphernalia of such a character. . . . This is another amiable Stewart comedy performance, an asset to any film venture."

New York Times, September 22, 1951

"To James Stewart's personal story of eccentric characters has now been added an appealing fuddy-dud. . . ."

The Greatest Show on Earth

DISTRIBUTOR: Paramount

RUNNING TIME: 151 minutes

CAST: Betty Hutton, Cornel Wilde, Charlton Heston, Dorothy Lamour, Gloria Grahame, James Stewart, Henry Wilcoxon, Lyle Bettger, Lawrence Tierney, Emmett Kelly, Cucciola, Antoinette Concello, John Ringling North, John Kellogg, John Ridgely, Frank Wilcox, Bob Carson, Lillian Albertson, Julia Faye, and Cast of the Ringling Bros.-Barnum & Bailey Circus

146 The Films of James Stewart

With Emmett Kelly in *The Greatest Show on Earth*

PRODUCER: Cecil B. DeMille
DIRECTOR: Cecil B. DeMille
ASSOCIATE PRODUCER: Henry Wilcoxon
SCREEN PLAY: Frederic M. Frank, Barre Johnson, Theodore St. John
PHOTOGRAPHY: George Barnes, Peverell Marley, Wallace Kelly
EDITOR: Anne Bauchens
CIRCUS MUSICAL AND DANCE NUMBERS: John Murray Anderson
SCORE: Victor Young
SONGS: Victor Young, Ned Washington, John Ringling North, E. Ray Goetz, Henry Sullivan, John Murray Anderson
REVIEWED: 12-13-51
RELEASED: 1-2-52

SYNOPSIS:

Brad (Charlton Heston) is the tough boss of a circus who puts the welfare of the circus above everything else. Holly (Betty Hutton) the aerialist is in love with Brad, but he doesn't have time for romance. The Great Sebastian (Cornel Wilde), great trapeze artist and lover that knows no boundaries, joins the circus and he and Holly's aeriel duels become a big drawing card for the Big Top.

In *The Greatest Show on Earth*

Sebastian has an eye for Holly, who is still trying to get Brad's attention.

Angel (Gloria Grahame) works dangerously with elephants and has her eye on Sebastian and Klaus (Lyle Bettger), the elephant trainer, becomes insanely jealous. Sebastian is seriously injured while performing and Holly feels she pushed him too far, is responsible for the accident, and agrees to marry him. Klaus is still jealous of Angel's shenanigans, and leaves the circus, causes a spectacular train crash, and is killed in the process. Brad is seriously injured and is pinned in the wreckage.

Buttons (Stewart) is a clown who has never been seen without his makeup and is actually a physician wanted for the mercy killing of his wife. He has to decide whether to gamble to save Brad's life. He does and is arrested by a detective (Henry Wilcoxon). Holly rallies the circus and leads the troupe for the next day's show. Brad realizes Holly is the girl he loves and needs and Angel and Sebastian are married.

Newsweek, January 21, 1952
"Undoubtedly the most foolish aspect of the narrative casts James Stewart as a sweet, sad clown. . . ."

With Betty Hutton and Emmett Kelly in *The Greatest Show on Earth*

New York Herald Tribune, January 11, 1952

"James Stewart has a minor role as a clown with a dark past hiding his identity behind the grinning make-up which he never takes off in the picture. He is good enough in his make-believe job to tour with the circus this spring."

Variety, January 2, 1952

"James Stewart is woven into the picture as an extraneous but appealing plot element."

Bend of the River

DISTRIBUTOR: Universal
RUNNING TIME: 91 minutes
CAST: James Stewart, Arthur Kennedy, Julia Adams, Rock Hudson, Lori Nelson, Jay C. Flippen, Stepin Fetchit, Henry Morgan, Chubby Johnson, Howard Petrie, Frances Bavier, Jack Lambert, Royal Dano, Frank Chase, Cliff Lyon, Frank Ferguson
PRODUCER: Aaron Rosenberg
DIRECTOR: Anthony Mann
SCREEN PLAY: Borden Chase
AUTHOR: Bill Gulick
PHOTOGRAPHY: Irving Glassberg
EDITOR: Russell Schoengarth
MUSIC: Hans J. Salter
REVIEWED: 1-15-52
RELEASED: 1-22-52

SYNOPSIS:

Glyn McLyntock (Stewart) is a former Missouri border raider who rescues Emerson Cole (Arthur Kennedy) from being lynched as a horse thief. McLyntock has signed on as a guide for a party of fruit farmers heading for Oregon and he is joined by Cole. On the way they lead the wagon train against a tribe of Shoshone Indians. Once in Portland the leader of the farmers, Jeremy Baile (Jay C. Flippen) gets Tom Hendricks (Howard Petrie) to arrange transportation up river for the necessary food for the winter.

The party reaches their destination up river by riverboat and builds a settlement. When the supplies do not arrive, McLyntock and Baile ride to Portland and find a gold rush has turned it into a boom town. Hendricks will not turn over the supplies. A gun battle follows and McLyntock and party get away on the riverboat with their property.

The lure of gold is too much for Cole, who leads a revolt against McLyntock when miners offer to buy the supplies and cattle. Cole

With Arthur Kennedy and Rock Hudson in *Bend of the River*

With Arthur Kennedy in *Bend of the River*

In *Bend of the River*

With Julia Adams and Arthur Kennedy in *Bend of the River*

holds Baile and his daughter, Laura (Julie Adams), captive and McLyntock follows the wagon train of supplies and gets it back. McLyntock has a bitter battle with Cole in the river and finally drowns him. Baile and his daughter accept McLyntock as a truly reformed highwayman and welcome the wagonload of supplies that will allow them to build fertile farms in their new home.

Catholic World, April, 1952
"As the ne'er-do-wells, James Stewart and Arthur Kennedy are often so persuasive that they have you believing all of the manufactured complications of the plot."

New York Times, April 10, 1952
"The distinction of 'Bend of the River' . . . two colorful performances by Arthur Kennedy and James Stewart.
". . . Both actors are first-rate performers when it comes to slinging guns and giving a general impression of cryptic personalities."

New York Herald Tribune, April 10, 1952
". . . Stewart is every inch the Western hero. . . ."

Carbine Williams

DISTRIBUTOR: Metro-Goldwyn-Mayer
RUNNING TIME: 90 minutes
CAST: James Stewart, Jean Hagen, Wendell Corey, Carl Benton Reid, Paul Stewart, Otto Hulett, Rhys Williams, Herbert Heyes, James Arness, Porter Hall, Fay Roope, Ralph Dumke, Leif Erickson, Henry Corden, Frank Richards, Howard Petrie, Stuart Randall, Dan Riss, Bobby Hyatt
PRODUCER: Armand Deutsch
DIRECTOR: Richard Thorpe
STORY AND SCREENPLAY: Art Cohn
PHOTOGRAPHY: William Mellor
EDITOR: Nowell P. Kimlin
REVIEWED: 4–10–52
RELEASED: 4–21–52

SYNOPSIS:
Marsh Williams (Stewart) is a prohibition-era North Carolina metalworker who adds to his income by making moonshine. He is convinced everyone has a right to do this. When he and his companions are raided by a group of Revenue agents one of the agents is killed during a shooting scrap. Even though it is unknown who fired the shot, Marsh's wife, Maggie (Jean Hagen) talks him into giving himself up. The trial results in a hung jury for first degree

Carbine Williams 153

In *Carbine Williams*

With Jean Hagen in *Carbine Williams*

In *Carbine Williams*

With Wendell Corey in *Carbine Williams*

murder and a retrial could send Williams to the chair, so he pleads guilty to a charge of second degree murder and starts serving 30 years in prison.

The prison warden, Capt. H. T. Peoples (Wendell Corey), allows Williams to work in the machine shop making guns from his own ideas. Williams is a stubborn and confused man and he rebels against prison authority. He spends time on a chain gang and also spends 30 days in "the hole." When not rebelling, though, he does have the talent to improve firearms and he conceives the short-stroke piston and invents the Army's 30 M-1 carbine. Over a 6-year period, 8,000,000 carbines later went overseas in WW II. For his deeds he is pardoned after serving eight years in prison.

Library Journal, June 1, 1952

"There is something throat catching in the way James Stewart gives the role his full sympathy and understanding."

Newsweek, May 26, 1952

". . . David Marshall Williams (simply and effectively played by James Stewart) . . . ."

Saturday Review, May 3, 1952

"What consistency there is to the film comes from the performances of James Stewart as Williams and Wendell Corey as a hard but sympathetic prison warden."

Time, May 12, 1952

"As the mountaineer, gangling James Stewart lopes easily through his role."

New York Herald Tribune, May 8, 1952

"Stewart's performance is in large part responsible for holding 'Carbine Williams' on a fairly realistic level."

New York Times, May 8, 1952

". . . James Stewart plays the title role in his customary gaunt and earnest fashion."

The Naked Spur

DISTRIBUTOR: M-G-M
RUNNING TIME: 91 minutes
CAST: James Stewart, Janet Leigh, Ralph Meeker, Robert Ryan, Millard Mitchell
PRODUCER: William H. Wright
DIRECTOR: Anthony Mann
SCREEN PLAY: Sam Rolfe, Harold Jack Bloom

With Millard Mitchell, Robert Ryan, Janet Leigh, Ralph Meeker in *Naked Spur*

With Janet Leigh in *Naked Spur*

The Naked Spur

With Janet Leigh in *Naked Spur*

ART DIRECTOR: Cedric Gibbons, Malcolm Brown
CINEMATOGRAPHER: William Mellor
EDITOR: George White
REVIEWED: 1-21-53
RELEASED: 2-6-53

SYNOPSIS:
Howard Kemp (Stewart) comes to Colorado to hunt for Ben Vandergroat (Robert Ryan) an escaped killer with a $5,000 price dead or alive. Kemp needs the money to regain some land he lost while fighting in the Civil War. Vandergroat has a female companion, Lina Patch (Janet Leigh), who knows him as a friend of the family and wants to go to California with Vandergroat since all her relatives are dead.

In the mountains Kemp runs into an aging prospector (Millard Mitchell) and a dishonorably discharged Union soldier (Ralph Meeker). They locate Vandergroat on a rocky hill and capture him and his companion. When the others learn that Kemp is not a lawman, as they first thought, they declare themselves partners and want their share of the reward money. Vandergroat is to be

With Robert Ryan, Ralph Meeker, Janet Leigh, Millard Mitchell in *Naked Spur*.

delivered to Abilene which is still seven days away by trail. Vandergroat feels his only chance is to badger the three until they are fighting among themselves for the full reward. He taunts them and several conflicts occur between the trio. Vandergroat also persuades Lina to compete for both Kemp and the Union soldier's affections. Before reaching their destination the prospector, Union soldier and Vandergroat are killed, Lina falls in love with Kemp and persuades him to go to California with her and forget about the reward.

Library Journal, February 15, 1953
   "The five players all turn in excellent performances."

Variety, January 14, 1953
   "The forthright story-telling, probably too raw and brutal for some theatregoers has excellent performances from its five stars headed by James Stewart."

Thunder Bay

DISTRIBUTOR: Universal

Thunder Bay

RUNNING TIME: 103 minutes
CAST: James Stewart, Joanne Dru, Gilbert Roland, Dan Duryea, Jay C. Flippen, Marcia Henderson, Robert Monet, Antonio Moreno, Henry Morgan
PRODUCER: Aaron Rosenberg
DIRECTOR: Anthony Mann
AUTHOR: Michael Hayes (from an idea by George W. George and George F. Slavin)
SCREEN PLAY: Gil Doud, John Michael Hayes
ART DIRECTOR: Alexander Golitzen, Richard H. Riedel
CINEMATOGRAPHER: William Daniels
EDITOR: Russell Schoengarth
REVIEWED: 5-5-53
RELEASED: August 1953

SYNOPSIS:

Steve Martin (Stewart) and Johnny Gambi (Dan Duryea) are oil wildcatters who arrive in Port Felicity, Louisiana. They are broke, but Steve has invented a stormproof drilling platform. He persuades Kermit MacDonald (Jay C. Flippen), an oil company

With Joanne Dru in *Thunder Bay*

With Gilbert Roland, Jay C. Flippen, Dan Duryea, Marcia Henderson in *Thunder Bay*

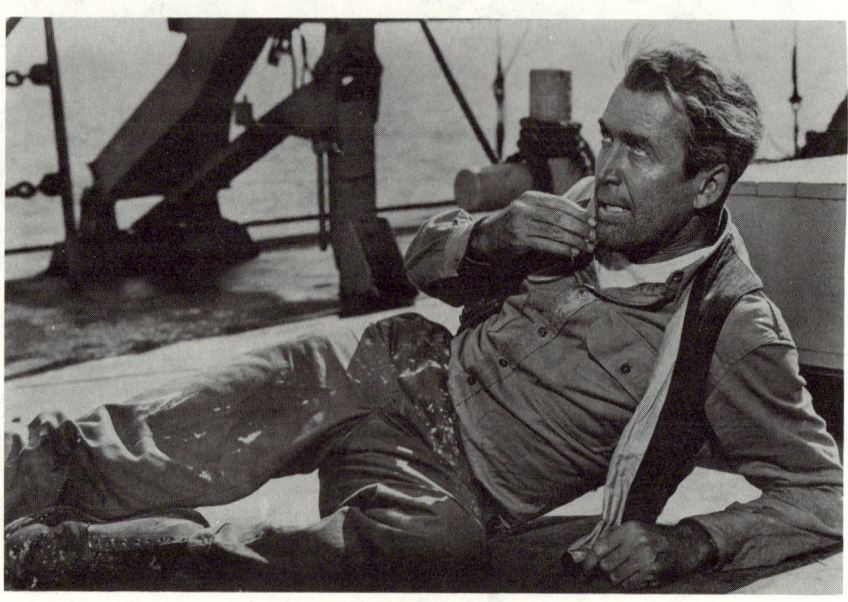

In *Thunder Bay*

In *Thunder Bay*

president, to invest a fortune to drill for oil in the harbor even though the oil company's future will be at stake.

Up to now shrimp fishing has been the town's sole enterprise and the fishermen have been having a tough time the past few weeks locating shrimp. They are convinced drilling for oil and the necessary blasting will only make matters worse. Several violent outbursts occur between the fishermen and the oil crews. To make matters worse, two sisters, Stella Rigaud (Joanne Dru) and Francesca Rigaud (Marcia Henderson), fall for Martin and Gambi. Martin is able to keep things fairly well under control until Francesca's jealous boyfriend tries to dynamite the rig during a hurricane and dies in the attempt. Most of the villagers then try to destroy the offshore rig. Time and money is running out but oil is discovered just in time. It also uncovers a shrimp bed and tensions are then eased.

New York Times, May 21, 1953

"James Stewart is properly tough, harried, begrimed and laconic as the indomitable wildcatter whose dream finally comes true."

Variety, May 6, 1953

"Stewart moves easily through his role as the stalwart, steadfast member of the adventuring pair."

The Glenn Miller Story

DISTRIBUTOR: Universal
RUNNING TIME: 115 minutes
CAST: James Stewart, June Allyson, Charles Drake, George Tobias, Henry Morgan, Frances Langford, Louis Armstrong, Gene Krupa, Ben Pollack, The Archie Savage Dancers, The Modernaires, Marion Ross, Irving Bacon, Kathleen Lockhart, Barton MacLane, Sig Ruman, Phil Harris, James Bell, Katherine Warren
PRODUCER: Aaron Rosenberg
DIRECTOR: Anthony Mann
AUTHORS: Valentine Davies, Oscar Brodney
PHOTOGRAPHY: William Daniels
EDITOR: Russell Schoengarth
DANCE DIRECTOR: Ken Williams
MUSICAL DIRECTOR: Joseph Gershenson
MUSICAL ADAPTATION: Henry Mancini
REVIEWED: 12-10-53
RELEASED: 1-6-54

SYNOPSIS:

This is the story of one of America's most popular bandleaders,

With June Allyson in *The Glenn Miller Story*

With June Allyson in *The Glenn Miller Story*

In *The Glenn Miller Story*

Glenn Miller, who created a new sound in music and died at the height of his popularity.

Glenn (Stewart) always had a consuming ambition to play the trombone and score music. He meets his future wife, Helen (June Allyson), at the University of Colorado and his sincerity and humility win her over. He later gets a job with the band of Ben Pollock (played by himself) and later works with a broadway pit crew. He spends his wedding night at a Harlem jazz session with Louis Armstrong, Gene Krupa, Cozy Cole, and others.

He takes lessons in musical theory and finds a friend in a Boston dance-hall operator, Si Schribman (George Tobias). He eventually becomes the recognized King of dance bands. He enlists in the Army and revolutionizes Army band music with his swinging versions. In mid-December of 1944 in a wartime English channel flight to prepare for a Paris concert for the troops, his plane disappeared, but he left his mark in the memories of millions of music fans.

Catholic World, February, 1954
  "Glenn is impersonated faithfully by James Stewart."

In *The Glenn Miller Story*

New Yorker, February 20, 1954

"In the film, James Stewart, who has the central role, goes about his work with an engaging air of bland good humor, and handles his trombone with convincing ease."

Newsweek, February 1, 1954

"The studio would seem to have gotten over its primary hazard by casting James Stewart as Miller. If any Hollywood star can simulate Miller's modest demeanor, Stewart, while not looking particularly like the maestro, is the man."

New York Herald Tribune, February 11, 1954

"James Stewart plays the role of the scholarly looking band leader with discretion and clarity and the shy good humor which clings to most of his roles."

New York Times, February 11, 1954

"Mr. Stewart and Miss Allyson in their roles—the gentle ease, the solid form of their strong acting—that puts the living throb into the film. It is they who make genuine the tender sentiments that are worked in behind the songs. This is a wonderful achievement, of which they and their associates may be proud."

Rear Window

DISTRIBUTOR: Paramount
RUNNING TIME: 112 minutes
CAST: James Stewart, Grace Kelly, Wendell Corey, Thelma Ritter, Raymond Burr, Judith Evelyn, Ross Bagdasarian, Georgine Darcy, Sara Berner, Frank Cady, Jesslyn Fax, Rand Harper, Irene Winston, Harris Davenport, Marla English, Bess Flowers
PRODUCER: Alfred Hitchcock
DIRECTOR: Alfred Hitchcock
SCREEN PLAY: John Michael Hayes
AUTHOR: Cornell Woolrich
PHOTOGRAPHY: Robert Burks
EDITOR: George Tomasini
REVIEWED: 7-9-54
RELEASED: 7-13-54

SYNOPSIS:

Jeff (Stewart) is a photographer for a big picture magazine who is laid up in his Greenwich Village apartment with a broken leg. Having nothing to do he passes the time by observing his neighbors with binoculars, since all of the apartment windows face a common courtyard. Seen through the lenses are Miss Lonely Hearts (Judith

With Wendell Corey and Grace Kelly in *Rear Window*

Evelyn), an aging spinster who entertains imaginary boy friends; a pair of newlyweds; a song writer (Ross Bagdasarian); a ballerina, Miss Torso (Georgine Darcy); and the most interesting of all, Lars Thorwald (Raymond Burr), a salesman with an invalid wife.

Jeff is frequently visited by his fiancee, Lisa Fremont (Grace Kelly), a beautiful high-fashion publicist whom he likes to have around but won't marry since he doesn't feel she could cope with his kind of life. Jeff notices that the salesman who had been patiently nursing his complaining wife suddenly is making trips in the rain as late as 2 A.M., carrying his sample suitcase. The next day he doesn't go into the wife's bedroom and the blinds in the bedroom are drawn. He mentions this to Lisa and she is at first skeptical of foul play. Jeff's nurse, Stella (Thelma Ritter), also is brought into the act, and when Jeff observes the salesman wrapping a saw and a carving knife in newspaper they are all sure that he has killed his wife.

Jeff confides in his friend, Police Lieutenant Thomas J. Doyle (Wendell Corey), but Doyle doesn't buy the foul play theory and tells Jeff to mind his own business.

With Grace Kelly in *Rear Window*

Rear Window

With Grace Kelly in *Rear Window*

With Thelma Ritter and Grace Kelly in *Rear Window*

170 The Films of James Stewart

Jeff, Lisa and Stella set out to try to trap the murderer, with Lisa actually getting into the salesman's apartment. The salesman finally realizes Jeff is on to him and comes to his apartment. Jeff tries to fight him off in the darkness with a barrage of flashbulbs, but is overpowered; but the New York police manage to get there in the nick of time, even though Jeff does fall from his window ledge, breaking the other leg.

Saturday Review, August 21, 1954

"And, as is generally the case with Hitchcock films, the studio has provided an expert and expensive cast, headed by James Stewart and Grace Kelly, which he has used with ingratiating effectiveness."

New York Herald Tribune, August 5, 1954

"There is a nervous, amiable vitality in Stewart's performance of the photographer."

Variety, July 14, 1954

"There's a very earthy quality to the relationship between Stewart and Miss Kelly. Both do a fine job of the picture's acting demands."

The Far Country

DISTRIBUTOR: Universal
RUNNING TIME: 97 minutes
CAST: James Stewart, Ruth Roman, Corinne Calvet, Walter Brennan, John McIntire, Jay C. Flippen, Henry Morgan, Steve Brodie, Royal Dano, Gregg Barton, Chubby Johnson, Eddy C. Waller, Robert Foulk, Eugene Borden, Allan Ray
PRODUCER: Aaron Rosenberg
DIRECTOR: Anthony Mann
AUTHOR: Borden Chase
SCREEN PLAY: Borden Chase
ART DIRECTORS: Bernard Herzbrun, Alexander Golitzen
MUSICAL DIRECTOR: Joseph Gershenson
CINEMATOGRAPHER: William Daniels
EDITOR: Russell Schoengarth
REVIEWED: 2-3-55
RELEASED: February 1955

SYNOPSIS:

Jeff Webster (Stewart) is a wrangler who also has a reputation for fancy shooting and his attitude is one of "live and let live." He and his partner Ben Tatum (Walter Brennan) herd their steers to Skagway, Alaska, by boat so they can buy a ranch in Utah that they have always wanted. When they get to Skagway, "the law" Mr.

In *The Far Country*

With Ruth Roman in *The Far Country*

With Ruth Roman in *The Far Country*

Gannon (John McIntire), grabs his herd. Jeff recaptures his beef and runs across the border to Dawson.

Ronda Castle (Ruth Roman), saloon-keeper in Dawson, takes a liking to Jeff and helps him. They realize Gannon and his men will come to town to get even. Jeff is undisturbed about this until they ambush him and Ben, and as Gannon's men leave Dawson, they kill Ben.

Jeff then goes after them and kills Gannon. Ronda, in trying to warn Jeff, is also killed. The turn of events change Jeff's attitude regarding his own business, seeking no help nor giving it. He returns to Skagway to seek Renee Vallon (Corinne Calvet) who had fallen in love with him upon his first visit.

New York Times, February 14, 1955
   "Count on James Stewart and a passel of tough types to lend conviction to a fairly standard adventure...."
   "James Stewart fits into the athletic proceedings to the manner born. Astride an arch-necked, majestic stallion, which he sits and rides well, he is an impressive figure."

Variety, January 26, 1955
   "Stewart and Brennan are completely at home in this type of film and handle their characters with the expected ease."

In *The Far Country*

Strategic Air Command

DISTRIBUTOR: Paramount
RUNNING TIME: 114 minutes
CAST: James Stewart, June Allyson, Frank Lovejoy, Barry Sullivan, Alex Nicol, Bruce Bennett, Jay C. Flippen, James Millican, James Bell, Rosemary DeCamp, Richard Shannon, John R. McKee, Henry Morgan, Don Haggerty, Glenn Denning, Anthony Warde, Strother Martin, Helen Brown, William Hudson, David Vaile, Vernon Rich, Harlan Warde, Robert House Peters, Jr., Henry Richard Lupino, William August Pullen, Stephen E. Wyman
PRODUCER: Samuel J. Briskin
DIRECTOR: Anthony Mann
SCREEN PLAY: Valentine Davies, Beirne Lay, Jr.
ART DIRECTORS: Hal Pereira, Earl Hedrick
MUSICAL DIRECTOR: Victor Young
CINEMATOGRAPHER: William Daniels
SPECIAL PHOTOGRAPHIC EFFECTS: John P. Fulton
AERIAL PHOTOGRAPHY: Thomas Tutwiler
PROCESS PHOTOGRAPHY: Farciot Edouart
EDITOR: Eda Warren
REVIEWED: 3-30-55
RELEASED: July 1955

SYNOPSIS:

The story is a tribute to the peacetime U.S. Air Force and the men of the Strategic Air Command's great long range bombers. The S.A.C. is the unit that can, if necessary, deliver nuclear bombs any place in the world on short notice.

Robert Holland (Stewart) is a $70,000, hot-shot third baseman for the St. Louis Cardinals who is recalled to the Air Force. After already serving in WW II he feels he has already done his share and should be allowed to play ball while he is still young enough to earn a good living in this manner. The Air Force is unyielding since it needs men of Lt. Colonel Holland's caliber to operate the B-36s and B-47s. His wife, Sally (June Allyson), is pregnant adding to his problems.

Lt. Colonel Holland is impressed with Commanding General Ennis C. Hawkes (Frank Lovejoy) who demands efficiency and security. He also is stirred by the enormity and alertness of S.A.C. and realizes its meaning to America's welfare. By the time his tour is up, he is ready to sign on with the Air Force as a professional. Sally rebels as S.A.C. takes hold of her husband, but she soon understands the importance of the program and shares his enthusiasm.

In *Strategic Air Command*

With June Allyson in *Strategic Air Command*

With Frank Lovejoy, James Millican, Bruce Bennett and Barry Sullivan in *Strategic Air Command*

With Jay C. Flippen and June Allyson in *Strategic Air Command*

New Yorker, April 30, 1955
"In the air, Mr. Stewart is every inch the lighthearted eagle, and various other birdmen . . . seem reassuringly capable."

Time, May 2, 1955
"Actor Stewart, as always, is an infinite gangle of charm."

Variety, March 30, 1955
"Stewart shows his usual professional competence, stirred by the enormity and alertness of SAC, becoming increasingly enraptured with its meaning to America's welfare and finally conveying believable sincerity in trying to convince his wife that SAC is his lifetime calling."

The Man from Laramie

DISTRIBUTOR: Columbia
RUNNING TIME: 104 minutes
CAST: James Stewart, Arthur Kennedy, Donald Crisp, Cathy O'Donnell, Alex Nicol, Aline MacMahon, Wallace Ford, Jack Elam,

In *The Man from Laramie*

With Cathy O'Donnell in *The Man from Laramie*

The Man From Laramie

John War Eagle, James Millican, Gregg Barton, Boyd Stockman, Frank de Kova
PRODUCER: William Goetz
DIRECTOR: Anthony Mann
AUTHOR: Thomas T. Flynn
SCREEN PLAY: Philip Yordan, Frank Burt
ART DIRECTOR: Cary Odell
MUSICAL DIRECTOR: Morris Stoloff
CINEMATOGRAPHER: Charles Lang, Jr.
EDITOR: William Lyon
REVIEWED: 7-1-55
RELEASED: August 1955

SYNOPSIS:

Will Lockhart (Stewart) rides from Laramie, Wyoming, to Coronado, New Mexico, with a mule team to deliver freight and find the man responsible for his younger brother's death. His brother was a cavalry officer killed by Apaches armed with automatic rifles and he's looking for the men who sold them the weapons. In town he meets Barbara Waggoman (Cathy O'Donnell), the niece of Alec Waggoman (Donald Crisp) who runs the town and owns most of the countryside.

After unloading his goods, Will moves on to some nearby salt lagoons, which are normally free for the asking, for a return trip. Waggoman's sadistic son, Dave (Alex Nicol), and his henchmen attack Will. Dave lassoes him, drags him through a bonfire, burns his wagons and shoots most of his mules. Will follows Dave into town, gives him a beating and then takes on the son's keeper, the foreman of Waggoman's ranch, Vic Hansbro (Arthur Kennedy).

Waggoman is a hard but fair man and pays Will for his damages and warns him to leave town. Will decides to stay despite his enemies as he has made friends with Barbara and a rival ranch owner, Kate Canaday (Aline MacMahon).

Later Will is framed for two murders including Dave's and Waggoman is out to kill him, but Will finally clears himself and exposes Vic as the killer and also as the man who sold the rifles to the Indians.

Newsweek, August 8, 1955

"The story is crammed with the usual Western gimmickery, but good acting makes its something more than the average outdoor show."

Saturday Review, July 30, 1955

"Stewart, through his gangling charm and innate honesty, never lets the hero become simply a stock figure."

In *The Man from Laramie*

New York Times, September 1, 1955

"Mr. Stewart is, as usual, atmospheric and incisive in his lean, heroic role."

The Man Who Knew Too Much

DISTRIBUTOR: Paramount
RUNNING TIME: 120 minutes
CAST: James Stewart, Doris Day, Brenda De Banzie, Bernard Miles, Ralph Truman, Daniel Gelin, Mognes Wieth, Alan Mowbray, Hillary Brooke, Christopher Olsen, Reggie Nalder, Richard Wattis, Noel Willman, Alix Talton, Carolyn Jones, Yves Brainville, Abdelhaq Chraibi, Betty Baskcomb, Leo Gordon, Patrick Aherne, Louis Mercier, Anthony Warde, Lewis Martin
PRODUCER: Alfred Hitchcock
ASSOCIATE PRODUCER: Herbert Coleman
DIRECTOR: Alfred Hitchcock
AUTHORS: Charles Bennett, D. B. Wyndham-Lewis
SCREEN PLAY: John Michael Hayes, Angus MacPhail
ART DIRECTORS: Hal Pereira, Henry Bumstead

In *The Man Who Knew Too Much*

With Doris Day, Bernard Miles and Brenda deBanzie in *The Man Who Knew Too Much*

With Doris Day, Christopher Olsen and Daniel Gelin in *The Man Who Knew Too Much*

The Man Who Knew Too Much

With Daniel Gelin in *The Man Who Knew Too Much*

MUSICAL DIRECTOR: Bernard Herrmann
CINEMATOGRAPHER: Robert Burks
EDITOR: George Tomasini
REVIEWED: 5-1-56
RELEASED: June 1956

SYNOPSIS:
   Ben McKenna (Stewart), an American surgeon is on vacation in MarraKech, Morocco, along with his wife, Jo (Doris Day), and son, Hank (Christopher Olsen). They make friends with a suspicious Frenchman, Louis Bernard (Daniel Gelin), and a friendly pair of Britons, Mr. and Mrs. Drayton (Bernard Mills and Brenda deBanzie), while seeing the sights. The next day while in a market place, a man in Arab clothing staggers toward them with a knife in his back. It is Louis Bernard who is really a French secret service agent. While dying he whispers to Ben an assassination plot that is to take place in London.
   Ben's son is kidnapped by the Drayton family to keep him from alerting the authorities. Ben and Jo go to London to try to track down the kidnappers and to try to prevent the assassination. They

realize their son's life is in grave jeopardy. The chase takes Ben to a taxidermist's shop, a chapel, and finally to Albert Hall, where the London Symphony Orchestra is performing. A bullet is to be fired into a visiting prime minister just as the cymbals clash. Ben and Jo manage in the nick of time to rescue their son and prevent the assassination.

Nation, June 9, 1956
"James Stewart and Doris Day, faultlessly groomed and as smooth as marbles, earn their high pay with perfect studio performances."

Saturday Review, May 26, 1956
". . . The cast is a fine one, the production is lavish, the settings are unusual. . . ."

Variety, May 2, 1956
"Stewart ably carries out his title duties."

The Spirit of St. Louis
DISTRIBUTOR: Warner Bros.
RUNNING TIME: 135 minutes

With Murray Hamilton in *The Spirit of St. Louis*

The Spirit of St. Louis

With Bartlett Robinson in *The Spirit of St. Louis*

CAST: James Stewart, Murray Hamilton, Patricia Smith, Bartlett Robinson, Marc Connelly, Arthur Space, Charles Watts
PRODUCER: Leland Hayward
DIRECTOR: Billy Wilder
SCREEN PLAY: Billy Wilder, Wendell Mayes
ADAPTATION: Charles Lederer
PHOTOGRAPHY: Robert Burks, J. Peverell Marley
REVIEWED: 2–15–57
RELEASED: 4–20–57

SYNOPSIS:
The story is Charles A. Lindbergh's solo flight across the Atlantic Ocean in 1927.

As an airmail pilot Lindbergh (Stewart) becomes aware of the possibility of a successful journey across the Atlantic. He struggles to find backers for his project. He finally gets a group of St. Louisans to promote the trip and a single-engine monoplane is built for the trip and named by the backers "The Spirit of St. Louis."

While waiting for rain to cease and during the flight itself, Lindbergh mentally remembers in a series of flashbacks his days of barnstorming with aerial circuses, flying mail, serving as an aviation

In *The Spirit of St. Louis*

In *The Spirit of St. Louis*

cadet and learning to fly by ear. To break the monotony of the trip he even chats with a horsefly that found its way into the cockpit.

As he flies alone over the Atlantic, he fights sleep and extreme fatigue, loses his compass for awhile and flies by the stars, and almost crashes when ice forms on his wings; he finally sights land and is mobbed when landing at Le Bourget, outside Paris, by a hysterical crowd. Finally, the unbelievable crowds and parade when he returns to New York show that he did indeed capture the imagination of the world.

National Parent-Teacher, April, 1957

"As played by James Stewart, in his usual sincere and disarming fashion, Lindbergh is an appealing but standardized hero."

Saturday Review, March 9, 1957

"Stewart has put a lot of effort into his characterization, and there are several scenes in which he is very likeable indeed."

Time, March 4, 1957

". . . Stewart, for all his professional, 48-year-old boyishness, succeeds almost continuously in suggesting what all the world sensed at the time: that Lindbergh's flight was not the mere physical adventure of a rash young 'flying fool,' but rather a journey of the spirit, in which, as in the pattern of all progress, one brave man proved himself for all mankind as the paraclete of a new possibility."

New York Times, February 22, 1957

"As Mr. Stewart plays him with his usual diffidence, he is mainly a type."

Night Passage

DISTRIBUTOR: Universal
RUNNING TIME: 90 minutes
CAST: James Stewart, Audie Murphy, Dan Duryea, Diane Foster, Elaine Stewart, Brandon de Wilde, Jay C. Flippen, Herbert Anderson, Robert J. Wilke, Hugh Beaumont, Jack Elam, Tommy Cook, Paul Fix, Olive Carey, James Flavin, Donald Curtis, Ellen Corby, John Day, Kenny Williams, Frank Chase, Harold Goodwin, Harold Tommy Hart, Jack C. Williams, Boyd Stockman, Henry Wills, Chuck Roberson, Willard Willingham, Polly Burson, Patsy Novak, Ted Mapes
PRODUCER: Aaron Rosenberg
DIRECTOR: James Neilson
SCREEN PLAY: Borden Chase
AUTHOR: Norman A. Fox

In *Night Passage*

In *Night Passage*

With Brandon de Wilde and Donald Curtis in *Night Passage*

192   The Films of James Stewart

In *Night Passage*

PHOTOGRAPHY: William Daniels
EDITOR: Sherman Todd
MUSIC: Dimitri Tiomkin
REVIEWED: 5-3-57
RELEASED: August 1957

SYNOPSIS:

Grant McLaine (Stewart) is an accordion-playing, disgraced railroad cop who is given another chance to get the railroad payroll safely to the railroad work-gang.

The gang leader of the outlaws is Whitey Harbin (Dan Duryea) and they are about to try their fourth attempt to get the payroll. Another member of the gang is the Utica Kid (Audie Murphy) who is McLaine's younger brother.

The thieves attempt to get the payroll, but McLaine gets young Joey Adams (Brandon deWilde) to hide the money. The highwaymen take Verna Kimball (Elaine Stewart) as hostage until the money makes its appearance. She is the wife of the railroad owner, Ben Kimball (Jay C. Flippen).

McLaine tries to talk his brother into leaving the gang, but to no avail. Finally, as McLaine seems trapped in a showdown with the gang, the Utica Kid has a change of heart and joins his brother against Whitey's gang of cutthroats. Whitey is killed and so is the Utica Kid, but McLaine manages to get the payroll to its destination.

New York Times, July 25, 1957

"Actually, it is the presence of Mr. Stewart in the show that gives it a personality above that of the average Western film."

"It is comforting to watch Mr. Stewart upholding the truthful and good."

Nation, August 17, 1957

". . . [Stewart] still has a nice boyish touch, and in fact it is a miracle how little the years have affected his nice boyish personality."

Vertigo

DISTRIBUTOR: Paramount
RUNNING TIME: 123 minutes
CAST: James Stewart, Kim Novak, Barbara Bel Geddes, Tom Helmore, Henry Jones, Raymond Bailey, Ellen Corby, Konstantin Shayne, Lee Patrick
PRODUCER: Alfred Hitchcock
DIRECTOR: Alfred Hitchcock
AUTHORS: Pierre Boileau, Thomas Narcejac
SCREEN PLAY: Alex Coppel, Samuel Taylor

With Kim Novak in *Vertigo*

With Tom Helmore in *Vertigo*

With Kim Novak in *Vertigo*

Vertigo

In *Vertigo*

ART DIRECTORS: Hal Pereira, Henry Bumstead
MUSIC: Bernard Herrmann
PHOTOGRAPHY: Robert Burks
EDITOR: George Tomasini
MAKE-UP: Wally Westmore
COSTUMES: Edith Head
REVIEWED: 5-14-58
RELEASED: 5-9-58

SYNOPSIS:

"Scottie" Ferguson (Stewart) is forced to retire from his job as a police lieutenant due to his fear of high places. An old college chum, Gavin Elster (Tom Helmore), induces him to trail his wife, Madeleine (Kim Novak). He explains that he is too busy to keep track of her due to his shipping company interests. Madeleine keeps wandering off and he feels she is drawn to suicide due to the influence of her great-grandmother who killed herself after going mad.

"Scottie" follows Madeleine for several days through scenic San Francisco, but they do not meet until he rescues her after she tries to drown herself in the bay. "Scottie" falls in love with her and fears for her life since she feels she is possessed by the spirit of her ancestor. Madeleine dreams of the Mission at San Juan Batista and "Scottie" takes her there hoping this will cure her. She climbs to the top of the Mission Tower and Scottie's acrophobia prevents him from following. He suddenly sees her body falling from the top and he suffers a mental breakdown. After his recovery, he meets a working girl named Judy (Kim Novak) who resembles Madeleine although her hair is a different color. She denies knowing "Scottie" or Madeleine but she had been hired by Elster to impersonate his *real* wife who was thrown from the tower by Elster. Scottie is suspicious and takes Judy to the tower. He forces himself to climb the stairs with her. She admits the truth about being hired by Elster and also tells "Scottie" that she really has fallen in love with him. A nun suddenly appears and startles Judy and she loses her balance and falls to her death.

Nation, June 14, 1958
"James Stewart carries out his detective and romantic assignments with easy grace and warmth."

Newsweek, June 2, 1958
"The production is slick, the performances are good, and San Francisco, the scene of the action, never looked prettier."

Time, June 16, 1958
". . . Actor Stewart is a fascinating old pro. . . ."

Bell, Book and Candle

DISTRIBUTOR: Columbia
RUNNING TIME: 103 minutes
CAST: James Stewart, Kim Novak, Jack Lemmon, Ernie Kovacs, Hermione Gingold, Elsa Lanchester, Janice Rule, Philippe Clay, Bek Nelson, Howard McNear, The Brothers Candoli, Wolfe Barzell, Joe Barry, Gail Bonney, Monty Ash
PRODUCER: Julian Blaustein
DIRECTOR: Richard Quine
SCREEN PLAY: Daniel Taradash
ART DIRECTOR: Cary Odell
MUSIC: George Duning
SONGS: Philippe Clay
EDITOR: Charles Nelson
PHOTOGRAPHY: James Wong Howe
MAKE-UP: Ben Lane
REVIEWED: 10-22-58
RELEASED: 10-9-58

SYNOPSIS:
Gillian Holroyd (Kim Novak) runs an art shop and when

With Kim Novak in *Bell, Book and Candle*

Shepherd Henderson (Stewart) walks into her shop one evening she says he's the man for her. On Christmas Eve, he spends a few hours in her apartment and falls in love with her. He postpones his Christmas Day wedding to Merle Kittridge (Janice Rule). What Shep doesn't know is that Gillian is a witch and with her black magic friends likes to walk through doors, jam telephones, turn street lights off and on and cause havoc with traffic. She has used her powers to put Shep under a spell although she is, as all witches, incapable of love.

Gillian has a brother Nicky (Jack Lemmon) who is helping an alcoholic author, Sidney Redlitch (Ernie Kovacs), write a book on Manhattan witches. Gillian asks Nicky to give up the book, but he refuses and states he will tell Shep what she really is. Gillian decides to tell Shep herself and he goes to Mrs. De Pass (Hermione Gingold) the super-witch of them all to break Gillian's spell. Gillian's aunt Queenie (Elsa Lanchester) manages to get the couple back together again. Shep sees Gillian blush and cry and he realizes love has turned her into a human being since a true witch can do neither.

198 The Films of James Stewart

With Hermione Gingold in *Bell, Book and Candle*

In *Bell, Book and Candle*

With Elsa Lanchester, Jack Lemmon, Kim Novak and Ernie Kovacs in *Bell, Book and Candle*

Good Housekeeping, January, 1959
". . . and James Stewart, the latter again master of the chuckling kind of dry comedy for which he has been famed all these years."

Newsweek, December 8, 1958
". . . and Jimmy Stewart, of course, always plays Jimmy Stewart."

Anatomy of a Murder

DISTRIBUTOR: Columbia
RUNNING TIME: 160 minutes
CAST: James Stewart, Lee Remick, Ben Gazzara, Arthur O'Connell, Eve Arden, Kathryn Grant, Joseph N. Welch, Brooks West, George C. Scott, Murray Hamilton, Orson Bean, Alexander Campbell, Joseph Kearns, Russ Brown, Howard McNear, Ned Wever, Jimmy Conlin, Ken Lynch, Don Ross, Lloyd Le Vasseur, Royal Beal, John Qualen, James Waters, Duke Ellington
PRODUCER: Otto Preminger
DIRECTOR: Otto Preminger
AUTHOR: Robert Traver

With Kathryn Grant in *Anatomy of a Murder*

SCREEN PLAY: Wendell Mayes
MUSIC: Duke Ellington
PHOTOGRAPHY: Sam Leavitt
EDITOR: Louis R. Loeffler
SET DECORATION: Howard Bristol
MAKE-UP: Del Armstrong, Harry Ray
REVIEWED: 6-26-59
RELEASED: 6-19-59

SYNOPSIS:

A bartender is murdered in a small Michigan city by Army Lieutenant Frederick Manion (Ben Gazzara). Manion claims he committed the crime because the bartender had beaten and raped his wife, Laura (Lee Remick). She substantiates her husband's story and although not admissible as evidence, a lie-detector bears her out; but a medical examination does not. She hires a former prosecuting attorney, Paul Biegler (Stewart), to defend her husband even though he is not particularly ambitious and is not used to saving clients. It is a challenge for Biegler. The deceased had been well-liked while Laura is well known as an easy mark for any-

With Lee Remick and Ben Gazzara in *Anatomy of a Murder*

With Arthur O'Connell in *Anatomy of a Murder*

With Ben Gazzara and Arthur O'Connell in *Anatomy of a Murder*

one. The prosecutor (George C. Scott) points out that Laura had probably been a willing partner with the bartender and Manion had beaten the truth out of her—which would account for her bruises—and then in a jealous rage went after her lover. He further states she is committing perjury to save her husband. Biegler has an able assistant who knows all about the law—when he's sober—in Parnell McCarthy (Arthur O'Connell). With his help they locate the records of an old trial where the accused had been acquitted on the grounds that he acted on an "irresistible impulse." Also in Biegler's favor is the victim's illegitimate daughter, Mary Pilant (Kathryn Grant), who takes the stand. Biegler wins the case and Manion is cleared of the crime. Another "irresistible impulse" takes place when Biegler tries to collect his fee. He finds that Manion and Laura have skipped town.

New Republic, July 13, 1959
   "The cast includes the never-varying James Stewart, giving more or less the same sturdy, boyish performance he gave in his very first film."

New Yorker, July 11, 1959
   ". . . James Stewart, in the role of the defense lawyer, has abandoned his customary delayed adolescent style, and once Mr. Premin-

ger permits him to get on with it, comes up with a most engaging performance."

Newsweek, July 13, 1959

". . . He uses Jimmy Stewart for the central role of the small-town defense lawyer, a part that looks tailor-made for his special talents of personality."

Saturday Review, July 11, 1959

". . . the marvelously equivocal portraits provided in *Anatomy of a Murder* by James Stewart, Lee Remick, Ben Gazzara, and George Scott reveal complexities in character such as rarely are seen on the American screen."

Time, July 13, 1959

"The actors—particularly Stewart and Remick—handle themselves like the glossy professionals they are."

The FBI Story

DISTRIBUTOR: Warner Bros.
RUNNING TIME: 149 minutes
CAST: James Stewart, Vera Miles, Murray Hamilton, Larry Pennell, Nick Adams, Diane Jergens, Jean Willes, Joyce Taylor, Victor Millan, Parley Baer, Fay Roope, Ed Prentiss, Robert Gist, Buzz Martin, Kenneth Mayer, Paul Genge, Ann Doran, Forrest Taylor
PRODUCER: Mervyn LeRoy
DIRECTOR: Mervyn LeRoy
SCREEN PLAY: Richard L. Breen, John Twist
PHOTOGRAPHY: Joseph Biroc
ART DIRECTOR: John Beckman
SET DECORATOR: Ralph S. Hurst
EDITOR: Philip W. Anderson
MUSIC: Max Steiner
SOUND: M. A. Merrick
MAKE-UP: Gordon Bau
ASSISTANT DIRECTORS: David Silver, Gil Kissel
REVIEWED: 9-12-59
RELEASED: October 1959

SYNOPSIS:

Chip Hardesty (Stewart) is a member of the poorly organized FBI in 1924. His future bride Lucy (Vera Miles) agrees to marry him if he gives up this career and becomes a lawyer. He agrees but wants to make a trip to Washington to meet the newly appointed head of the FBI, J. Edgar Hoover. He is so impressed with him he

In *The FBI Story*

With Larry Pennell in *The FBI Story*

In *The FBI Story*

does not resign. Lucy realizes she can not change his mind and they marry.

During the next few years Chip helps in fighting the Ku Klux Klan of the South, traps the murderers of the oil-rich Osage Indians in Oklahoma and aids in rounding up the notorious gangsters of the 30s. One of the gangsters, Baby Face Nelson, kills Chip's partner and closest friend, Sam Crandall (Murray Hamilton).

Chip and Lucy are constantly on the move and with three children it is more than Lucy can stand and she leaves him; but finally she returns. During WW II he fights German espionage agents in South America and his son Mike (Buzz Martin) is killed in action. After the war Chip works against the Communists in New York. After a long and distinguished career he receives his final assignment . . . teaching young recruits the responsibility of being a G-man.

Films in Review, October, 1959

"James Stewart well plays the role of the FBI agent who is a fine and noble human."

Variety, August 19, 1959

"Stewart gives a restrained performance, wry and intelligent, completely credible as the film covers a span of about 25 years to show both the fledgling agent and the older man."

The Mountain Road

DISTRIBUTOR: Columbia
RUNNING TIME: 102 minutes
CAST: James Stewart, Lisa Lu, Glenn Corbett, Henry Morgan, Frank Silvera, James Best, Rudy Bond, Mike Kellin, Frank Maxwell, Eddie Firestone, Alan Baxter, Leo Chen, Bill Quinn, Peter Chong, P. C. Lee
PRODUCER: William Goetz
DIRECTOR: Daniel Mann
AUTHOR: Theodore White
SCREEN PLAY: Alfred Hayes
MUSIC: Jerome Moross
ASSISTANT DIRECTOR: Irving Moore
REVIEWED: 3-23-60
RELEASED: June 1960

SYNOPSIS:
China is torn apart by the war in 1944. A U.S. Army Major named Baldwin (Stewart) volunteers for his first command. He heads an eight-man demolition team that is the last garrison of an airfield in southeast China, and the Japanese are only 40 miles away.

In *The Mountain Road*

In *The Mountain Road*

In *The Mountain Road*

Their task is to destroy vital bridges and roads preventing the advancement of the Japanese. Major Baldwin takes this command to learn of the nature of power and believes he has the ability to use it wisely.

They blow up a mountain bridge and are joined by two Chinese: Madame Sue-Mei Hung, a Radcliffe graduate (Lisa Lu) and General Kwan (Frank Silvera). The destruction of the bridge leaves thousands of Chinese homeless and she resents Major Baldwin's indifference to the situation. His attitude worsens as one of his men is trampled to death by starving Chinese when he offers a case of rations. Later, Chinese military deserters kill two more of his men and Major Baldwin has a whole village destroyed, killing hundreds of innocent women and children. Although Madame Sue-Mei Hung and Baldwin have had a strong attraction toward one another even through their differences this action causes her to leave him. He later admits he misused his power but learned from her compassion even in war time.

Variety, March 23, 1960

"As played by James Stewart, the American major holds the film together."

Two Rode Together

With Lisa Lu and Frank Silvera in *The Mountain Road*

New York Times, June 30, 1960

"It's reassuring to watch a real pro like Jimmy Stewart holding together a mild, little war sermon like *The Mountain Road*."

Two Rode Together

DISTRIBUTOR: Columbia
RUNNING TIME: 109 minutes
CAST: James Stewart, Richard Widmark, Shirley Jones, Linda Cristal, Andy Devine, John McIntire, Paul Birch, Willis Bouchey, Henry Brandon, Harry Carey Jr., Olive Carey, Mae Marsh, Jeannette Nolan, Ken Curtis, Chet Douglas, Annelle Hayes, David Kent, Anna Lee, Ford Rainey, Woody Strode, John Qualen, O. Z. Whitehead, Cliff Lyons, Frank Baker, Ruth Clifford, Ted Knight, Sam Harris
PRODUCER: Stan Sheptner
DIRECTOR: John Ford
AUTHOR: Will Cook
SCREEN PLAY: Frank Nugent
MUSIC: George Duning

With Richard Widmark, Shirley Jones, Linda Cristal and John McIntire in *Two Rode Together*

With Henry Brandon and Richard Widmark in *Two Rode Together*

Two Rode Together

With Linda Cristal in *Two Rode Together*

ASSISTANT DIRECTOR: Wingate Smith
REVIEWED: 6-19-61
RELEASED: July 1961

SYNOPSIS:

Guthrie McCabe (Stewart) is a grafting, cynical Texas marshal who has a 10 percent piece of everything in a panhandle dust hole during the 1880s. The Comanches have taken dozens of white captives and McCabe is asked to help Cavalry Lt. Jim Gary (Richard Widmark) rescue the prisoners. McCabe refuses until he is offered $500 for each captive.

McCabe and Gary obtain Running Wolf (David Kent), a white boy raised as an Indian, in exchange for two rifles and also Elena (Linda Cristal), a young Mexican who is the squaw of warrior Stone Calf (Woody Strode). As they prepare to leave camp McCabe has trouble with Stone Calf and kills him.

When they return to the fort Mrs. McCandless (Jeanette Nolan) claims Running Wolf as her long lost son. When she frees him of his bonds, he kills her. The settlers lynch Running Wolf but before he dies it is discovered he is actually Marty Purcells's (Shirley Jones) brother. Lt. Gary is in love with Marty. Elena is shunned by

With Richard Widmark in *Two Rode Together*

the officers' wives and McCabe loses his job to his deputy. McCabe and Elena leave the fort to search for a better life.

Time, July 28, 1961
"Stewart plays the heavy convincingly."

Variety, June 21, 1961
"Stewart far and away cops histrionic honors, employing and projecting all the casual charm, assurance and personal magnetism he has developed in the course of a long and distinguished career. It's a performance sure to delight his many fans."

X-15

DISTRIBUTOR: United Artists
RUNNING TIME: 107 minutes
CAST: David McLean, Charles Bronson, Ralph Taeger, Brad Dexter, Kenneth Tobey, James Gregory, Mary Tyler Moore, Patricia Owens, Lisabeth Hush, Stanley Livingston, Lauren Gilbert, Phil Dean, Chuck Stanford, Patty McDonald, Mike MacKane, Robert Dornam, Frank Watkins, Barbara Kelley, Darlene Hendricks and narrated by James Stewart

The Man Who Shot Liberty Valance 215

PRODUCERS: Henry Sanicola, Tony Lazzarino
EXECUTIVE PRODUCER: Howard W. Koch
DIRECTOR: Richard D. Donner
SCREEN PLAY: Tony Lazzarino, James Warner Bellah
PHOTOGRAPHY: Carl Guthrie
MUSIC: Nathan Scott
ART DIRECTOR: Rolland M. Brooks
SET DECORATOR: Kenneth Schwartz
EDITOR: Stanley Rabjohn
MAKE-UP: Beans Pondell
ASSISTANT DIRECTORS: Russ Haverick, Jay Sandrich
REVIEWED: 11–10–61
RELEASED: November 1961

James Stewart narrates this film concerning the rigors of the X-15 research work at Edwards Air Force Base, California.

The Man Who Shot Liberty Valance
DISTRIBUTOR: Paramount

With Woody Strode, John Wayne and Vera Miles in *The Man Who Shot Liberty Valance*

With Vera Miles in *The Man Who Shot Liberty Valance*

With Robert F. Simon, Andy Devine, Ken Murray, and Edmond O'Brien in *The Man Who Shot Liberty Valance*

RUNNING TIME: 123 minutes
CAST: James Stewart, John Wayne, Vera Miles, Lee Marvin, Edmond O'Brien, Andy Devine, Woody Strode, Ken Murray, John Qualen, Jeanette Nolan, Lee Van Cleef, Strother Martin, John Carradine, Willis Bouchey, Carleton Young, Denver Pyle, Robert F. Simon, O. Z. Whitehead, Paul Birch, Joseph Hoover
PRODUCER: Willis Goldbeck
DIRECTOR: John Ford
SCREEN PLAY: James Warner Bellah, Willis Goldbeck
PHOTOGRAPHY: William H. Clothier
MUSIC: Cyril Mockedge
ART DIRECTORS: Hal Pereira, Eddie Imazu
EDITOR: Otho Lovering
SOUND: Philip Mitchell
MAKE-UP: Wally Westmore
ASSISTANT DIRECTOR: Wingate Smith
REVIEWED: 4–11–62
RELEASED: April 1962

SYNOPSIS:
The year is 1910. Senator Ranse Stoddard (Stewart) and his wife, Hallie (Vera Miles), come to the small community of Shinbone

With Edmond O'Brien in *The Man Who Shot Liberty Valance*

to attend the funeral of Tom Doniphan (John Wayne). Senator Stoddard's visit was not scheduled and a curious reporter asks why he came. The Senator tells the following story:

Many years ago when he was a young lawyer in Shinbone he stood against the notorious gunman, Liberty Valance (Lee Marvin). The only other two men in the town that were not afraid of the ruthless Valance were Tom Doniphan, and a drunken but courageous newspaper editor, Dutton Peabody (Edmond O'Brien). Tom was a well-known and honored rancher in love with Hallie, then a young waitress.

Valance taunts Ranse into a duel after Ranse is elected as a delegate to a territorial convention. Hallie pleads with Tom to intervene since she knows Ranse can not handle a gun. Tom refuses since he has grown tired of Ranse's foolhardy bravery. Late that night on the dark main street Ranse and Valance face each other, fire several shots and afterwards Valance is dead and Ranse wounded. Ranse becomes famous and is nominated for Congress due to his notoriety as "The Man Who Shot Liberty Valance." He decides to refuse the nomination as he can not adjust to a career built on a killing. When Tom hears this he comes forward and confesses that he killed Valance due to his love for Hallie. This was the force that carried Ranse to the U.S. Senate and a brilliant career.

Variety, April 11, 1962

"Stewart and Wayne do what comes naturally in an engagingly effortless manner."

Films in Review, May, 1962

"The 'Ford actors'—Wayne, Stewart, Qualen, Strode and others—all performed on cue."

New York Times, May 24, 1962

"Mr. Stewart makes an effectively fumbling but indomitable lawyer, who values honesty as much as justice."

Mr. Hobbs Takes a Vacation

DISTRIBUTOR: 20th Century-Fox
RUNNING TIME: 116 minutes
CAST: James Stewart, Maureen O'Hara, Fabian, John Saxon, Marie Wilson, Reginald Gardiner, Lauri Peters, Valerie Varda, Lili Gentle, John McGiver, Natalie Trundy, Josh Peine, Minerva Urecal, Michael Burns, Richard Collier, Peter Oliphant, Thomas Lowell, Stephen Mines, Dennie Whitcomb, Michael Sean
PRODUCER: Jerry Wald
DIRECTOR: Henry Koster

With Valerie Varda in *Mr. Hobbs Takes A Vacation*

With Maureen O'Hara and Minerva Urecal in *Mr. Hobbs Takes A Vacation*

With Maureen O'Hara in *Mr. Hobbs Takes A Vacation*

SECOND UNIT DIRECTOR: William Witney
SCREEN PLAY: Nunnally Johnson
PHOTOGRAPHY: William C. Mellor
MUSIC: Henry Mancini, Johnny Mercer
ART DIRECTOR: Jack Martin Smith, Malcolm Brown
SET DECORATOR: Walter M. Scott, Stuart A. Reiss
EDITOR: Marjorie Fowler
MAKE-UP: Ben Nye
ASSOCIATE PRODUCER: Marvin A. Gluck
ASSISTANT DIRECTOR: Joseph E. Rickards
REVIEWED: 5-16-62
RELEASED: July 1962

SYNOPSIS:
Roger Hobbs (Stewart) is hoping for a quiet vacation. His wife, Peggy (Maureen O'Hara), decides that the family needs a month at a seashore cottage. Things go wrong from the beginning. The cottage turns out to be such a crumbling monstrosity that their cook, Brenda (Minerva Urecal), leaves in a huff. Son Danny (Michael Burns) is too involved with TV to try the beach; daughter Katey

In *Mr. Hobbs Takes A Vacation*

(Lauri Peters) has braces on her teeth and refuses to go out; daughter Susan (Natalie Trundy) arrives with her family and unemployed husband Stan (Jose Peine); daughter Janie (Lili Gentle) and her husband (John Saxon) also have their problems when Byron becomes interested in a bikini worn by Marika (Valerie Varda).

Peggy even has her hands full with one of the yacht club set, Reggie McHugh (Reginald Gardiner), a self-styled Romeo. Gradually Mr. Hobbs tries to restore family harmony.

He repairs the house's horrendous pump, guides a small boat through a foggy bank, winning son Danny's respect. He introduces Katey to a good looking Joe (Fabian). He further helps Stanley land a job by entertaining a drunken bird-watcher (John McGiver) and his wife (Marie Wilson), manages to lure Stanley away from Marika and with some fancy romancing of his own gets Peggy's mind off of Reggie.

The vacation is finally over with Hobbs much relieved until he finds Peggy has leased the cottage for the next summer.

Variety, May 16, 1962

"The picture has its staunchest ally in Stewart, whose acting instincts are so remarkably keen that he can instill amusement into scenes that otherwise threaten to fall flat."

How the West Was Won

DISTRIBUTOR: Metro-Goldwyn-Mayer
RUNNING TIME: 155 minutes
CAST: Carroll Baker, Lee J. Cobb, Henry Fonda, Carolyn Jones, Karl Malden, Gregory Peck, George Peppard, Robert Preston, Debbie Reynolds, James Stewart, Eli Wallach, John Wayne, Richard Widmark, Brigid Bazlen, Walter Brennan, David Brian, Andy Devine, Raymond Massey, Agnes Moorehead, Harry Morgan, Thelma Ritter, Mickey Shaughnessy, Russ Tamblyn, Tudor Owens, Barry Harvey, Jamie Ross, Kimm Charney, Brian Russell, Claude Johnson, Jerry Holmes, Rudolph Acosta, Willis Bouchey and narrated by Spencer Tracy
PRODUCER: Bernard Smith
DIRECTORS: Henry Hathaway, John Ford, George Marshall
SCREEN PLAY: James R. Webb
PHOTOGRAPHY: William H. Daniels, Milton Krasner, Charles Lang, Jr., Joseph LaShelle
ART DIRECTORS: George W. Davis, William Ferrari, Addison Hehr
SET DECORATORS: Henry Grace, Don Greenwood Jr., Jack Mills
EDITOR: Harold F. Kress

With Carroll Baker, Kimm Charney, Brian Russell and Karl Malden in *How the West Was Won*

MAKE-UP: William Tuttle
ASSISTANT DIRECTORS: George Marshall Jr., William McGarry, Robert Saunders, William Shanks, Wingate Smith
MUSIC: Alfred Newman
ASSOCIATE: Ken Darby
REVIEWED: 11-7-62
RELEASED: Special

SYNOPSIS:

Zebulon (Karl Malden) and Rebecca Prescott (Agnes Moorehead) are attracted by the prospect of free land in the West in the 1830s. They take their family, daughters Eve (Carroll Baker), and Lilith (Debbie Reynolds) and two sons down the Ohio River by raft. They run into fur trapper Linus Rawlings (Stewart) who rescues them from a band of river pirates led by Colonel Hawkins (Walter Brennan). Later the raft capsizes during a dangerous trip through some rapids. Both parents are drowned. Linus catches up with the Prescott family and asks for Eve's hand. They build a farm on the spot where her parents are buried.

Lilith goes on to St. Louis and becomes an entertainer in dance

In *How the West Was Won*

halls. Several years later an elderly admirer leaves her a California gold mine. She joins Roger Morgan's (Robert Preston) Westward-bound wagon train and falls in love with a fortune-hunting gambler, Cleve Van Valen (Gregory Peck). He leaves Lilith when he finds her gold mine is worthless, but he has a change of heart and they seek their fortune in booming San Francisco.

The Civil War breaks and Linus is killed in action. Eve's son, Zeb (George Peppard), joins the Union Army. He befriends a deserter (Russ Tamblyn) from the Confederate Army, but later kills him as he tries to shoot both General Grant (Harry Morgan) and General Sherman (John Wayne). The war ends and Zeb returns home only to find his mother has died. He joins a cavalry troop protecting railroad workers from the Indians. With the help of buffalo hunter Jethro Stuart (Henry Fonda), Zeb keeps peace with the Indians for awhile. Mike King (Richard Widmark), the railroad foreman, finally riles the Indians with his ruthlessness and they start a buffalo stampede and destroy the railroad camp. Zeb is disgusted, resigns his position and becomes an Arizona marshal. In the late 1880s he is visited by the now widowed Lilith. He is forced to leave the reunion when his enemy, Charlie Gant (Eli Wallach),

With Carroll Baker in *How the West Was Won*

In *How the West Was Won*

attempts to hold up the train carrying a shipment of gold. After a furious gun battle involving a runaway train, Zeb kills Gant and returns to Aunt Lilith and his family.

Variety, November 7, 1962
  "Stewart has some fine, if typical, moments in his scenes, and he gets involved in a magnificently directed fight. It's a no-holds barred punch-up in which anything goes."

Take Her, She's Mine

DISTRIBUTOR: 20th Century-Fox
RUNNING TIME: 98 minutes
CAST: James Stewart, Sandra Dee, Audrey Meadows, Robert Morley, Philippe Forquet, John McGiver, Robert Denver, Monica Moran, Jenny Maxwell, Cynthia Pepper, Maurice Marsac, Irene Tsu, Charla Doherty, Marcel Hillaire, Charles Robinson, Janine Grandel.
PRODUCER: Henry Koster

With Sandra Dee in *Take Her, She's Mine*

In *Take Her, She's Mine*

Take Her, She's Mine

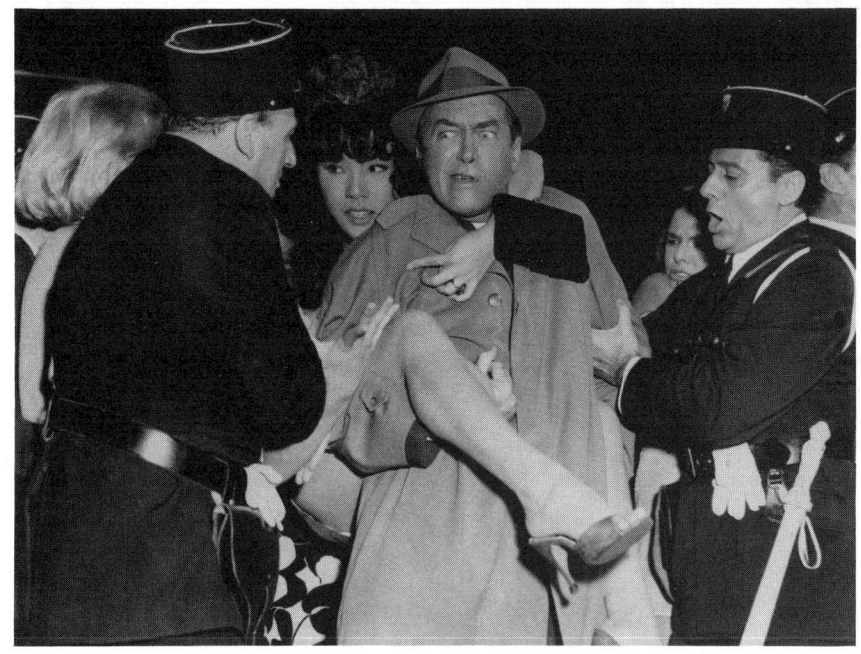

In *Take Her, She's Mine*

DIRECTOR: Henry Koster
SCREEN PLAY: Nunnally Johnson
PHOTOGRAPHY: Lucien Ballard
MUSIC: Jerry Goldsmith
ART DIRECTOR: Jack Martin Smith, Malcolm Brown
SET DECORATOR: Walter M. Scott, Stuart A. Reiss
EDITOR: Marjorie Fowler
SOUND: W. D. Flick
MAKE-UP: Ben Nye
ASSISTANT DIRECTOR: Joseph E. Rickards
REVIEWED: 11-14-63
RELEASED: 10-9-63

SYNOPSIS:

Lawyer Frank Michaelson (Stewart) and his wife, Anne (Audrey Meadows), are worried about the reputation of their daughter, Mollie (Sandra Dee), when they send her away to college. Boys were their only concern, but they soon have more to worry about when Mollie becomes embroiled with "Ban the Bomb" demon-

With Audrey Meadows in *Take Her, She's Mine*

strators and beatnik folk singers. Frank gets into several embarrassing situations while trying to help her.

Mollie goes to Paris on an art scholarship and things become even worse. Frank sees her name linked with Henri Bonnet (Philippe Forquet), a young painter, and he flies to France. He only creates more havoc when he is accidentally arrested during a police raid on a second-rate tavern.

Mollie is in love with Henri and introduces him to her father at a costume ball. Frank's Daniel Boone costume falls apart and he falls into the Seine. Despite all the misfortunes Mollie and Henri are married and Frank returns home to begin worrying over his younger daughter, Liz (Charla Doherty).

Variety, October 16, 1963

"Middle aged and more elderly filmgoers figure to relate to the character played so infectiously by their old favorite, Stewart."

Cheyenne Autumn

DISTRIBUTOR: Warner Bros.

Cheyenne Autumn

With Arthur Kennedy in *Cheyenne Autumn*

RUNNING TIME: 156 minutes
CAST: Richard Widmark, Carroll Baker, Karl Malden, Sal Mineo, Dolores Del Rio, Ricardo Montalban, Gilbert Roland, Arthur Kennedy, Patrick Wayne, Elizabeth Allen, John Carradine, Victor Jory, Mike Mazurki, George O'Brien, Sean McClory, Judson Pratt, Carmen D'Antonio, Ken Curtis, John Qualen, Shug Fisher, Nancy Hsueh, and James Stewart, Edward G. Robinson
PRODUCER: Bernard Smith
DIRECTOR: John Ford
ASSOCIATE DIRECTOR: Ray Kellogg
SCREEN PLAY: James R. Webb
MUSIC: Alex North
EDITOR: Otho Lovering
ART DIRECTOR: Richard Day
PHOTOGRAPHY: William H. Clothier
SET DECORATOR: Darryl Silvera
ASSISTANT DIRECTORS: Wingate Smith, Russ Saunders
REVIEWED: 10-7-64
RELEASED: December 1964

SYNOPSIS:

In the 1870s the government's reckless and pitiless reservation policy causes 1000 Cheyenne Indians to move from their homeland in Wyoming to a meager Oklahoma reservation. Disease and starvation takes its toll after one year of waiting for Federal aid and the number has been reduced to 286. The survivors are determined to travel the 1500 miles to their Yellowstone way of life.

Deborah Wright (Carroll Baker) is a sympathetic Quaker school teacher and she joins them. They are pursued by her fiance, Captain Thomas Archer (Richard Widmark), and the U.S. Cavalry who hope to bring them back without bloodshed. A quick-tempered brave named Red Shirt (Sal Mineo) starts several skirmishes and several soldiers are killed. The newspapers play it up big, calling the Cheyennes "marauding savages."

Tension mounts and Wyatt Earp (Stewart) and Doc Holliday (Arthur Kennedy) are pressured into leading a war party. Earp intentionally leads his drunken posse in the wrong direction and remains on the trail until the pressure subsides.

Winter comes and the Cheyenne divide into two bands—half continue the journey but the rest surrender to the brutal Captain Wessel (Karl Malden). Wessel plans to march the Indians back

With John Carradine, Judson Pratt and Arthur Kennedy in *Cheyenne Autumn*

With Chuck Roberson and Ken Curtis in *Cheyenne Autumn*

to Oklahoma, but the Indians revolt, killing him, and escape into the snow. Captain Archer has gone back to Washington to seek the help of Carl Schurz, the Secretary of the Interior (Edward G. Robinson). The Indians are caught and are about to be massacred by troops when Archer arrives with the Secretary. A treaty is formulated and the Cheyenne return to their home. Once home Red Shirt and Chief Little Wolf (Ricardo Montalban) settle an old dispute over Little Wolf's wife and Red Shirt is killed. Peace is restored and Deborah and Archer remain with the surviving Indians.

Newsweek, January 11, 1965

"Richard Widmark and James Stewart are at least themselves, do what they always do, and earn their money. Stewart, in a parody of a poker game, provides the picture's only feeble twitch of life."

Time, January 8, 1965

". . . there is a hilarious cameo performance by James Stewart who pops up in Dodge City for an irrelevant but clearly intentional spoof of Wyatt Earp."

Dear Brigitte

DISTRIBUTOR: 20th Century-Fox
RUNNING TIME: 100 minutes

With Ed Wynn in *Dear Brigitte*

With Cindy Carol in *Dear Brigitte*

Dear Brigitte

With Fabian, Glynis Johns, Billy Mumy, and Cindy Carol in *Dear Brigitte*

CAST: James Stewart, Fabian, Glynis Johns, Cindy Carol, Billy Mumy, John Williams, Jack Kruschen, Charles Robinson, Howard Freeman, Jane Wald, Alice Pearce, Jesse White, Gene O'Donnell, Ed Wynn, Brigitte Bardot
PRODUCER: Henry Koster
DIRECTOR: Henry Koster
SCREEN PLAY: Hal Kanter (Based on the novel *Erasmus with Freckles* by John Haase)
MUSIC: George Duning
DIRECTOR OF PHOTOGRAPHY: Lucien Ballard
ASSISTANT DIRECTOR: Fred R. Simpson
COSTUMES: Moss Mabry
REVIEWED: 1-28-65
RELEASED: January 1965

SYNOPSIS:

Robert Leaf (Stewart) is a poet and professor at California College who is devoted to the arts and hates science. He lives with his wife, Vina (Glynis Johns), and family on an old ferryboat. For evening relaxation the family members entertain themselves with

With Glynis Johns in *Dear Brigitte*

their own music. His eight-year-old son, Erasmus (Billy Mumy), plays the cello, but is tone-deaf and switches to painting; but he is color-blind. While Professor Leaf is trying to find some interest for his son he learns much to his chagrin that Erasmus is a mathematical genius. He tries to keep it a secret, but to no avail.

Soon Erasmus is helping his sister, Pandora (Cindy Carol), and her boyfriend, Kenneth (Fabian), with their homework, but only for a fee. Kenneth and a friend soon have Erasmus handicapping horses since Pandora wants to marry a millionaire. Erasmus's only real interest is Brigitte Bardot, to whom he has been writing letters, and he tries to have enough money from his fees for a trip to Europe to visit her.

A con man, Peregrine Upjohn (John Williams), hears of Erasmus and makes a proposition to Professor Leaf to finance a foundation for students interested in humanities by having Erasmus handicap horses. The money starts piling in but Erasmus then balks until he can visit Brigitte in Paris as she asked in a reply to his letters. Professor Leaf and Erasmus visit Brigitte and return. Upjohn plans one long shot and then is going to abscond with the money. The horse wins and as Upjohn is cashing in he is intercepted by an internal revenue agent. Professor Leaf explains the money is for a non-profit organization and claims the money for the foundation. Life on the ferryboat then returns to as near normal as possible.

Variety, February 3, 1963

"James Stewart is perfect in characterization of the idealistic voice in academic wilderness, as nuclear labs and computer setups encroach upon his domain of arts and letters at a mythical modern university."

Shenandoah

DISTRIBUTOR: Universal

RUNNING TIME: 120 minutes

CAST: James Stewart, Doug McClure, Glenn Corbett, Patrick Wayne, Rosemary Forsyth, Phillip Alford, Katharine Ross, Charles Robinson, James McMullan, Tim McIntire, Eugene Jackson, Jr., Paul Fix, Denver Pyle, George Kennedy, James Best, Tom Simcox, Berkeley Harris, Harry Carey, Jr., Kevin Hagen, Dabbs Greer, Kelly Thordsen, Strother Martin

With Paul Fix, Phillip Alford and Tim McIntire in *Shenandoah*

In *Shenandoah*

Shenandoah 239

With Rosemary Forsyth, Katharine Ross, Phillip Alford, James McMullan, Glenn Corbett, Tim McIntire, Patrick Wayne and Charles Robinson in *Shenadoah*

PRODUCER: Robert Arthur
DIRECTOR: Andrew V. McLaglen
SCREEN PLAY: James Lee Barrett
DIRECTOR OF PHOTOGRAPHY: William H. Clothier
MUSIC: Frank Skinner
COSTUMES: Rosemary Odell
ASSISTANT DIRECTOR: Terence Nelson
REVIEWED: 4-14-65
RELEASED: August 1965

SYNOPSIS:
The Civil War has been an occasional rifle shot distantly heard on 500 acres of good rich dirt in Virginia farm country. The autocratic widowed owner, Charlie (Stewart), maintains that the conflict between the states does not concern his large household. Charlie is a man of conviction and fortitude and has never had a slave and he feels justifiable pride in the fact that he and his well-disciplined, devoted family have worked long and hard for everything they own. He refuses to take sides with either Army.

The war becomes real to them when the youngest of his six strapping sons, Boy (Phillip Alford), wears a Confederate cap he has found and is captured by Yankee troops. He is only spared from death by his former playmate, a freed slave. With four of his sons and his daughter, Charlie goes searching for him. The family's isolation is over as they are drawn deeper and deeper into the conflict. They endure separation, fear and death and share the violence and sorrows of the war. Charlie and the remaining members of the family return home without Boy and ride off for Sunday services at the village church. The lost son hobbles in on makeshift crutches and the family is reunited, but still wondering about the futility of war.

Newsweek, August 23, 1965

"What Stewart himself achieves must be a source of some discouragement as well as instruction for the young, unskilled actors working with him. He is far from young. His role of pater-familias is more tired than his eyes. Yet Stewart compels belief with his strength and simplicity."

Flight of the Phoenix

DISTRIBUTOR: 20th Century-Fox
RUNNING TIME: 147 minutes
CAST: James Stewart, Richard Attenborough, Peter Finch, Hardy Kruger, Ernest Borgnine, Ian Bannen, Ronald Fraser, Christian Marquand, Dan Duryea, George Kennedy, Gabriele Tinti, Alex Montoya, Peter Bravos, William Aldrich, Barrie Chase
PRODUCER: Robert Aldrich
DIRECTOR: Robert Aldrich
SCREEN PLAY: Lukas Hellar
AUTHOR: Elleston Trevor
PHOTOGRAPHY: Joseph Biroc
MUSIC: Frank DeVol
ASST. DIRECTORS: William F. Sheehan, Cliff Coleman, Alan Callow
REVIEWED: December 1966
RELEASED: December 1966

Bush pilot Frank Towns (Stewart) is enroute to Bengazi in a rickety old twin-engine plane. The cargo plane is carrying oil-company workers to a new outpost, Also on board is an alcoholic navigator, Lew Moran (Richard Attenborough); a young German plane designer, Heinrich Dorfmann (Hardy Kruger); a French doctor, Dr. Renaud (Christian Marquand); a British Army captain, Harris (Peter Finch) and his sergeant, Watson (Ronald Fraser).

With Ernest Borgnine in *The Flight of the Phoenix*

With Richard Attenborough and Hardy Kruger in *The Flight of the Phoenix*

With Ronald Fraser, Dan Duryea and George Kennedy on the set of *The Flight of the Phoenix*

In *The Flight of the Phoenix*

The plane crashes in the Sahara and Towns accepts full responsibility even though the disaster was largely due to the negligence of the drunken navigator. Two passengers are killed and another severely injured.

At first the men assume they will be quickly rescued. Then they realize they will not and must survive through their own efforts. Towns gets together with Captain Harris and Sergeant Watson to organize some means of survival. The water supply is almost gone and Captain Harris and another survivor, Carlos (Alex Montoya), set out to try to find help. An American oil driller, Trucker Cobb (Ernest Borgnine), suffering from a mental collapse, follows them. Towns goes after them only to find Cobb dead.

Heinrich suggests to the survivors that with his engineering ability they can fashion a smaller plane out of the wreckage. Towns doesn't believe the plane will work and fights him all the way. Captain Harris returns without help and Towns realizes Heinrich's plan is their only hope. After several days of backbreaking work and exposure to the sun, sand and each other the plane is finally constructed. They cannot all fit aboard and the men strap themselves on the wings. After several false starts Towns finally manages to get the strange aircraft off the ground and to safety.

New Yorker, February 12, 1966
"James Stewart, Hardy Kruger, Richard Attenborough, Peter Finch and Ronald Fraser are all splendid in their roles."

Saturday Review, January 29, 1966
". . . [Director Robert] Aldrich helps remind us what a splendid actor James Stewart can be."

Time, February 4, 1966
"James Stewart in his best role of recent years."

Variety, February, 1966
"Stewart is particularly effective in underplaying his character."

The Rare Breed

DISTRIBUTOR: Universal
RUNNING TIME: 108 minutes
CAST: James Stewart, Maureen O'Hara, Brian Keith, Juliet Mills, Don Galloway, David Brian, Jack Elam, Ben Johnson, Hugh Carey, Jr., Perry Lopez
PRODUCER: William Alland
DIRECTOR: Andrew V. McLaglen
DIRECTOR OF PHOTOGRAPHY: William Clothier

With Juliet Mills in *The Rare Breed*

ASST. DIRECTORS: Terry Morse, Jr., Tom Schmidt
REVIEWED: 1-28-66
RELEASED: February 1966

SYNOPSIS:

Martha Evans (Maureen O'Hara) is the widow of a British cattle-breeder. She and her daughter, Hilary (Juliet Mills), are attending the 1884 St. Louis Stockman's Exposition in order to sell their prize white-faced Hereford bull, Vindicator. They feel their bull is just the thing for crossbreeding with the traditional lean, longhorn stock then prevalent in the West. Vindicator is sold and experienced cowhand Sam Burnett (Stewart) is given the task of delivering the animal to its purchaser in Dodge City.

The ladies insist on seeing it to its destination and they accompany Sam on the hazardous journey to Dodge City. Sam saves the ladies from stampedes, desperadoes and seduction and finally delivers the trio to the ranch of cattle baron Alexander Bowen (Brian Keith), the bull's new owner. Bowen feels the mother-daughter combination have eccentric ideas and scoffs at the idea that the hornless Hereford can withstand the cruel winter long enough to start a new dynasty, but he does turn Vindicator loose on the range.

In *The Rare Breed*

With Maureen O'Hara in *The Rare Breed*

With Maureen O'Hara and Juliet Mills in *The Rare Breed*

Bowen's ranch is a crumbling heap and as the winter passes the household reaps the benefit of Martha's gentle influence. When spring comes, Sam, who has fallen for Martha, searches the range to see if the animal has survived. He finally discovers the corpse of Vindicator, but he also finds a longhorn cow with a Hereford calf and realizes the "rare breed" has begun.

Variety, February 2, 1966
". . . it should be noted that Stewart's somewhat offbeat role is handled in topflight fashion right down to the happy ending. . . ."

Firecreek

DISTRIBUTOR: Warner Bros.-Seven Arts
RUNNING TIME: 104 minutes
CAST: James Stewart, Henry Fonda, Inger Stevens, Gary Lockwood, Dean Jagger, Ed Begley, Jay C. Flippen, Jack Elam, James Best, Barbara Luna, Jacqueline Scott, Brooke Bundy, J. Robert Porter, Morgan Woodward, John Qualen, Louise Latham, Athena Lorde, Harry "Slim" Duncan
PRODUCER: Philip Leacock
DIRECTOR: Vincent McEveety
SCREEN PLAY: Calvin Clements
MUSIC: Alfred Newman
EDITOR: William Ziegler
ART DIRECTOR: Howard Hollander
SOUND: Stanley Jones
ASSISTANT DIRECTOR: Jack Cunningham
MAKE-UP: Gordon Bau
SET DECORATOR: William L. Kuehl
REVIEWED: 1-16-68
RELEASED: 1-20-68

SYNOPSIS:

This is the story of a part-time sheriff suddenly faced with defending his town against a gang of freebooting adventurers from the Missouri range wars.

Minutes after the arrival of the adventurers in town, two of the gang, Earl (Gary Lockwood) and Drew (James Best), get into a wild brawl over Meli (Barbara Luna), a beautiful Indian girl. Earl is about to drown Drew in a horse-trough when farmer Johnny Cobb (Stewart) quietly calls a halt. Arthur (J. Robert Porter), a slow-thinking stable boy, informs them that farmer Cobb is the part-time sheriff. Larkin (Henry Fonda), the leader of the adventurers, certainly hadn't figured on any law being within 100 miles and

With Gary Lockwood, Henry Fonda, Jack Elam and Morgan Woodward in *Firecreek*

With Henry Fonda in *Firecreek*

With Dean Jagger, Ed Begley and Athena Lorde in *Firecreek*

certainly not a farmer-sheriff who draws $2.00 a month for maintaining law and order in a sleepy town.

Larkin, nursing a wound received during his travels, is resting at a boarding house run by Pittman (Jay C. Flippen) and his granddaughter, Evelyn (Inger Stevens). Evelyn bandages Larkin and tries to persuade him to reform. A subdued but powerful romantic interest develops between them.

After dark, Arthur hear a muffled cry from Meli's house and finds her struggling against Drew's advances. Arthur, brutally beaten in trying to defend Meli, accidentally kills Drew with the adventurer's own gun. Larkin's men accuse Arthur of murder and Cobb has to jail the stable-boy for his own protection. When Cobb is called away from town, the Larkin gang breaks into the jail and lynches Arthur.

Cobb returns to town and proclaims that he will see Larkin and his men hanged, which sets off a skirmish. A fierce battle ensues, with Larkin as the gang's sole survivor. Then, with both Cobb and Larkin wounded, the lawless adventurer and the farmer-sheriff face one another with guns drawn. Cobb attempts to reload his gun but Larkin shoots it out of his hand. When Cobb tries to pick up the gun, Larkin takes deliberate aim. He never fires the fatal shot, for he is killed by a shot from a boarding house window—a shot fired by Evelyn.

In *Firecreek*

Independent Film Journal

"The time-worn formula succeeds because of all-around solid performing by an expert cast, sparked by James Stewart's best acting in some years. It is his marvelous performance that give *Firecreek* its distinction."

Film Bulletin, February 5, 1968

"An exceptionally fine performance by the always reliable Stewart (worthy of an Academy Award nomination)."

Variety, January 24, 1968

"Stewart plays one of his typical slow-talking, honest rugged individuals."

Kansas City Star, January 28, 1968

"Stewart and Fonda give beautiful performances."

Bandolero!

DISTRIBUTOR: 20th Century-Fox
RUNNING TIME: 107 minutes
CAST: James Stewart, Dean Martin, Raquel Welch, George Kennedy,

252 The Films of James Stewart

Andrew Prine, Will Geer, Clint Ritchie, Denver Pyle, Tom Heaton, Rudy Diaz, Sean McClory, Harry Carey, Donald Barry, Guy Raymond, Jock Mahoney
PRODUCER: Robert L. Jacks
DIRECTOR: Andrew V. McLaglen
SCREEN PLAY: James Lee Barrett
AUTHOR: Stanley L. Hough
PHOTOGRAPHY: William H. Clothier
EDITOR: Folmar Blangsted
MUSIC: Jerry Goldsmith
ART DIRECTOR: Jack Martin Smith, Alfred Sweeney, Jr.
SOUND: Herman Lewis, David Dockendorf
ASST. DIRECTOR: Terry Morse, Jr.
REVIEWED: 5–28–68
RELEASED: 6–18–68

Dee Bishop (Dean Martin) leads a post-Civil War band of outlaws. Dee kills a rich rancher while holding-up a bank in a Texas town. This lands the gang in Sheriff Johnson's (George Kennedy) jail where they are waiting to be hanged.

With Dean Martin, Clint Richie, Sean McClory, Will Geer, and George Kennedy in *Bandolero!*

Bandolero!

With Dean Martin and Raquel Welch in *Bandolero!*

Mace Bishop (Stewart), Dee's older brother, waylays the itinerant hangman on his way to town and takes his place in order to help the gang escape. He requires the citizens to turn in their firearms until after the execution to avert any trouble. On the scaffold he slips Dee a gun and Sheriff Johnson is disarmed and the gang escapes. Mace has a streak of larceny in him as he slips into the bank and takes $10,000.

Sheriff Johnson leads the posse after the gang and is relentless in his pursuit. Maria (Raquel Welch), the murdered rancher's widow, was kidnapped by the outlaws. Sheriff Johnson is very interested in Maria. He refuses to turn back when it seems hopeless, due to his love for Maria.

The outlaws are followed into Mexico. Sheriff Johnson captures the Bishop brothers in an abandoned pueblo. A band of Mexicans attack Johnson and his men and the Sheriff releases Dee and Mace to help fight the bandits. Dee is killed in the skirmish. Mace gives up the loot to Sheriff Johnson and is also killed.

Variety, June 5, 1968

"Stewart and Kennedy have the advantage of talent and good definition in their roles."

A Selected Bibliography

1. "New Faces," E. Reed. *Theatre Arts Monthly.* April 1935.
2. "The Blade of Beverly Hills," *Collier's.* October 9, 1937.
   A story on the newcomer Jimmy Stewart as the boy next door. A synopsis of his early years, experience and views on life and marriage, his plans for the future.
3. "Mr. Smith Goes to Town," *Time.* July 24, 1944.
   36-year-old Lt. Col. James Stewart appointed Air Force Chief of Staff by Br. Gen. Ted Timberlake—a brief resume of his Air Force career, as a bomber-pilot instructor, administrative officer, and squadron leader.
4. "Life Comes Home with James Stewart," *Life.* September 24, 1945.
5. "Jimmy Stewart's Finest Performance," Col. Beirne Lay, Jr. *Saturday Evening Post.* December 8, December 15, 1945.
   Two-part article details Stewart's performance in the armed forces during the war years.
6. "Stewart Touch," *Newsweek.* December 30, 1946.
   Article discusses Stewart's desire to return to acting and reaffirm his status after having proven himself in the Air Force during the war. As the only actor in his family Stewart's type of acting became immediately popular and in teaming up with director Frank Capra—also returning from the war wondering whether he had lost his touch—he found a fine harmony exemplified in *It's A Wonderful Life.*
7. "Penrod in Hollywood," *Woman's Home Companion.* April 1947.
8. "American as Apple Pie," *Christian Science Monitor Magazine.* October 25, 1947.
9. "Target: Hollywood," *Collier's.* April 5, 1947.
   After five years in the service, Stewart feared he might be washed up in his career but he found he hadn't lost his touch. Also discusses the success of *It's A Wonderful Life.*
10. *Life.* September 20, 1948.
    Article is written about Leland Hayward and Stewart is prominently mentioned for his professional connection and friendship with Hayward.

A Selected Bibliography

11. "Jimmy Stewart is Married At Last," *Life*. August 22, 1949.
    Pictures and short write-up on Jimmy's marriage to Gloria Hatrick McLean.
12. "Jimmy Stewart hits the Jackpot," *Life*. December 4, 1950.
    Stewart hits the jackpot both careerwise and in society. He does a fine job with his movie roles in *Harvey* and *The Jackpot* and is introduced to Princess Margaret and the royal family.
13. *Time*. June 25, 1951
    Kelly and Judy Stewart, new born Stewart twins, were joined by Mrs. Stewart's two sons by her previous marriage for publicity photos.
14. "The Shyest Guy in Hollywood," Pete Martin, *Saturday Evening Post*. September 15, 1951.
    One of the famous series of articles by Martin is an interesting and illuminating interview with Stewart.
15. "Jimmy's Twins," *Collier's*. May 17, 1952.
16. "Jimmy Stewart tells what he Wants for his Family," *Parents Magazine*. July 1952.
17. *Life*. September 5, 1955.
    Article on the making of the movie *The Man Who Knew Too Much*. Between takes, Stewart was a tourist in Morocco.
18. "Lucky To Be Lindy," *Collier's*. March 30, 1956.
    Written by Stewart in association with Joseph Laitin, Stewart tells of his feelings while playing the role of Charles A. Lindbergh—how he learned the route, saw Lindy from afar and how fortunate he felt to be able to portray the famous aviator.
19. *Newsweek*. September 2, 1957.
    Lt. Gen. Emmett (Rosy) O'Donnell went before the Senate Armed Services Committee to ask that Stewart gets the star of a Brigadier General. By 11–2 the committee rejected Stewart's promotion under the opposition of Sen. Margaret Chase Smith who, it was suggested, was bitter because her administrative assistant was omitted.
20. "One Star for Jimmy," *Newsweek*. February 23, 1959.
    Summary of the 1957 controversy between Margaret Chase Smith of Maine and the Senate Committee over Stewart's promotion—previously, in the face of public opinion, Mrs. Smith proved her point. This time it seems Stewart has met the requirements and he supposedly will get his star.
21. "Lady Balks Again," *Newsweek*. March 3, 1959.
    Margaret Chase Smith is adamant in her opposition to Stewart's promotion. She still doesn't like his record and is convinced the Air Force is using reserve stars to win friends and influence people. She asked pointed questions—said she might reconsider.

22. "Star for a Star But . . ." *Newsweek.* July 22, 1959.
    Jimmy is finally promoted to Brigadier General—Smith and Senate committee voted yes on the Air Force promise to publicly announce his new assignment at "Public Information Headquarters," U.S.A.F., Washington, D.C.
23. *Ladies Home Journal.* May 1960.
    Short layout on the Stewarts' kitchen and its planning.
24. "This Was My Father," interview edited by F. Miller. *McCall's.* May 1964.
25. "James Stewart," edited by Pete Martin. *Saturday Evening Post.* Feb. 11, Feb. 18, Feb. 25, March 4, March 11, 1961.
    Excellent five part article written by Stewart in conjunction with Pete Martin; thorough analysis of Stewart's career as seen from his own point of view.
26. "The Respawnsibility of bein' J . . . Jimmy Stewart!", Peter Bogdanovich, *Esquire.* July 1966.
27. *Pete Martin Calls On . . .,* Pete Martin, New York: Simon and Schuster, 1962. Chapter XII, "Tall in the Saddle," contains a section on Stewart's career.
28. "James Stewart," William R. Sweigart, *Films in Review,* December, 1964.
29. *Nothing More to Declare,* John Clellon Holmes, New York: E. P. Dutton & Co., Inc., 1967.
30. *Variety.*